ODE · TO · LOVE

100 POEMS OF LOVE & LUST

ODE·TO·LOVE
100 POEMS OF LOVE & LUST

PORTICO

This edition published by
Portico Books
10 Southcombe Street
London
W14 0RA

An imprint of Anova Books Company Ltd

First published as *Homage to Eros* in Great Britain in 2005 by
Robson Books

ISBN   9781907554384

A CIP catalogue record for this book is available from the British
Library.

10 9 8 7 6 5 4 3 2 1

Printed and bound by CPI Mackays, Chatham, Kent, ME5 8TD

This book can be ordered direct from the publisher at
www.anovabooks.com

CONTENTS

INTRODUCTION

Two thousand and four hundred years ago Plato spoke of the ancient desire of man to make one of two. In so doing, I may add, he and/or she is likely to say, 'I love you'. No wonder those with the gift of language give homage to Eros by expanding on those three little words in one thousand and more surprising ways. 'If ever two were one, then surely we,' wrote the early American poet, Anne Bradstreet.

What a rich picking there is for an anthologist of love poems, of stories of enduring love and love lost. Not to mention wonderful confessions, often robustly comical, of pure lust, mainly by men, since in past centuries declarations of love or about love were generally a male preserve. Sometimes these declarations are sincere, gallant and heartfelt, the poets hymning the physical attributes and nature of their beloveds. Others speak more in lust than in love, flatter to deceive, hoping that their finely chosen sweet words will edge the adored one into their beds.

When I was a schoolboy I hardly responded to the domestic love poems that we were forced to read in successive chalky classrooms. I could not take seriously dead poets' confectionery words composed for whispering into inclined delicate ears: 'Thy teeth are like a flock of sheep, Cynthia'; 'Thy two breasts are like two young roes, Amarantha'; 'The smell of thy garments is like the smell of Lebanon, Chloris.' I did not believe those poets were genuinely smitten and I was too young to appreciate, as I do now, their playful eloquence. The best of flattery that I could stammer

1

in praise of my then current sixteen-year-old girl friend was, 'Oh you do look well, Lesbia.'

The first love poem that I truly found engaging was in the yellow-jacketed Poems for Spain (1940) edited by Stephen Spender and John Lehmann. The poem (which I have included in this anthology) was called 'Huesca'. It was written by John Cornford who, not yet 21 years old, was killed while fighting in the International Brigade against Franco's fascist forces. It was the last poem that he was to write. How poignant, I thought, his melancholy premonition of his own death:

And if bad luck should lay my strength
Into the shallow grave
Remember all the good you can;
Don't forget my love.

I memorised the poem and I can recite it still, and it moves me still – its poignant directness, the simplicity and economy of its language. It makes me think of the time and the place, the threat of the coming battle at Huesca, the young man who wrote it and the woman he wrote it to and how she probably read it after she learnt of his fate, read it in the privacy of her room, in a house, somewhere in England.

Later, I was to enjoy the great variety of love poems of different ages and of different countries, to listen to cries of 'Gather ye rosebuds while ye may' and 'My true love hath my heart and I have his' and 'My love bound me with a kiss' and 'Since there's no help, come, let us kiss and part' and 'Come live with me and be my love' and 'Let's contend no more, love' and 'Woman much missed how you call to me, call to me' and so many more.

The present anthology, as may be already inferred from the tone of this introduction, is a highly personal one: it does not attempt to be representative or academic. Simply, I have chosen one hundred love poems that I have enjoyed – famous poems as well as those perhaps hardly known even to the poetry-reading public. The poems range from 'The Song of Solomon' to masterworks by poets of our own time. I have selected relatively few translations for, as R S Thomas said, 'A translation is like a kiss through a handkerchief.' The American poet, Ramon Guthrie, put it in another way:

And there is amour and love
What either of them is I cannot say
except that they are not
identical
One of them is much more
something or other than the other:
They are as different as
to die and mourir
though how to define
their differences either only
Dieu knows or God sait.

Still I hope that the translations included here do read as if their original language was English, that the handkerchief is missing.

Love and Death, Eros and Thanatos, are two principal patrons of poetry and sometimes they join forces when a man or woman expresses feelings about the irrevocable loss of a loved one: 'All my life's bliss is in the grave with thee,' wrote Emily Brontë. There are a number of poems of regret and lament in this anthology, but there are many that celebrate sexual energy, the gaiety, the humour and seriousness of Eros.

Dannie Abse

The Song Of Solomon (10th century bc) is a dialogue between two smitten lovers. Nowhere else in the Bible is there such a passionate paean of praise for sexual love. No wonder later rabbis and priests attempted to tame its erotic content by interpreting the poem as an allegory of the love of Jehovah for Israel or the union of Christ with the church. It has been claimed that Solomon wrote the poems when he was a romantic youth though no hint of any author appears in the text. The style of the collection relates to love lyrics anciently used at marriage festivals in the Near East and is part of an oral tradition.

I am the rose of Sharon,
And the lily of the valleys.

As the lily among thorns,
So is my love among the daughters.

As the apple tree among the trees of the wood,
So is my beloved among the sons.
I sat down under his shadow with great delight,
And his fruit was sweet to my taste.
He brought me to the banqueting house,
And his banner over me was love.
Stay me with flagons, comfort me with apples:
For I am sick of love.
His left hand is under my head,
And his right hand doth embrace me.
I charge you, O ye daughters of Jerusalem,
By the roes, and by the hinds of the field,
That ye stir not up, nor awake my love, till he please.

The voice of my beloved! behold, he cometh
Leaping among the mountains, skipping upon the hills.
My beloved is like a roe or a young hart:
Behold, he standeth behind our wall,
He looketh forth at the windows,

Shewing himself through the lattice.
My beloved spake, and said unto me,
'Rise up, my love, my fair one, and come away.
For, lo, the winter is past,
The rain is over and gone;
The flowers appear on the earth;
The time of the singing of birds is come,
And the voice of the turtle is heard in our land;
The fig tree putteth forth her green figs.
And the vines with the tender grape give a good smell.
Arise, my love, my fair one, and come away.'

(This section of the Song of Solomon comes from the Authorised
Version of the Bible, 1611.)

Gaius Valerius Catullus (c. 84 bc–c. 54 bc), who is considered Rome's first major lyric poet, was born in Verona. Little is known about him but he probably left his home town for Rome when he was nineteen years of age, armed with introductions to Roman literary society. His poems to 'Lesbia' were addressed, in fact, to Clodia Metelli, who was well-born, rich and married. It is thought that Catullus's affair with her began before her husband's death. She was certainly a liberated and promiscuous lady whom Cicero said 'behaved like a prostitute'. That Catullus was smitten by her is evident from his sensual autobiographical poems.

TO LESBIA

Lesbia, let us live and let us love,
defy the severe tut-tutting elders
who advocate cold restraint, how all must die.

Our sun will set but will not always rise
so kiss me now, here in bed or heather,
before night's numb and endless slumber.

Then let us kiss again one thousand times,
then a hundred times, exceed a thousand more,
for each sweet kiss will another breed

until we do not know which who is who
and happily we'll confuse the number
to keep on kissing, kissing, kissing ever.

Ovid (c. 43 BC–AD 18) Publio Ovidius Naso, to give him his full name, a Latin poet of the Augustan age. He was 30 years old before he published his first book of poems, **Amores**, a collection of love poems addressed to a courtesan named Corinna. Ovid's poetry was admired by and influenced such poets as Chaucer, Spenser and Milton. In 1598, Francis Meres wrote, 'The sweete wittie soule of Ovid lives in the mellifluous and honey-tongued Shakespeare.'

FROM ELEGIES
TO CORINNA

In summer's heat and mid-time of the day
To rest my limbs upon a bed I lay;
One window shut, the other open stood,
Which gave such light as twinkles in a wood,
Like twilight glimpse at setting of the sun,
Or night being past and yet not day begun.
Such light to shamefast maidens must be shown,
Where they may sport, and seem to be unknown.
Then came Corinna in a long loose gown,
Her white neck hid with tresses hanging down:
Resembling fair Semiramis going to bed
Or Lais of a thousand wooers sped.
I snatched her gown; being thin, the harm was small,
Yet strived she to be covered therewithal.
And striving thus as one that would be cast,
Betrayed herself, and yielded at the last.
Stark naked as she stood before mine eye,
Not one wen in her body could I spy.
What arms and shoulders did I touch and see,
How apt her breasts were to be touched by me!
How smooth a belly under her waist saw I!
How large a leg, and what a lusty thigh!
To leave the rest, all liked me passing well;

I clinged her naked body, down she fell.
Judge you the rest; being tired she bade me kiss.
Jove send me more such afternoons as this.

Translated by Christopher Marlowe

FROM AMORES
(BOOK TWO)

I'd rather be in hell with one woman
than in heaven with all those sexless angels.

Sweet Corinna may deceive me and then we
quarrel – but oh what reconciliations!

True, Desire's lantern burns dimly sometimes
yet with a little oil it soon flares up.

You know how it is: a horse bolts suddenly
and, helpless, the rider tugs at the reins.

Or a yacht is driven back from the shore
when its sails are caught up in gusts of wind.

Well, Cupid's arrows know their own way home.
They feel more at home in me than in their quiver!

Life's on lease. Why settle for eight hours sleep
and ignore delightful, flighty Cupid?

Sleep's a rehearsal for undying Death.
There's time enough for nights of peace. So shoot

on, with one eye closed, mischievous boy,
let your arrows seek my heart forever.

Adapted by Dannie Abse

Li Po (AD 8th century) is generally believed to be the greatest of Chinese poets. He lived a courtly life and was not averse to drinking from 'The Wine-Cup'. Legend has it that while in a boat, intoxicated, he tried to embrace the reflection of the moon in the water and drowned. It was while working on literal Japanese versions of classical Chinese poems that Ezra Pound wrote 'The River Merchant's Wife' by Li Po (Rihaku). How much of this version is by Li Po and how much by Ezra Pound I am not qualified to say. It does not matter. It is a beautiful love poem.

THE RIVER MERCHANT'S WIFE:
A Letter

While my hair was still cut straight across my forehead
I played about the front gate, pulling flowers.
You came by on bamboo stilts, playing horse,
You walked about my seat, playing with blue plums.
And we went on living in the village of Chokan:
Two small people, without dislike or suspicion.

At fourteen I married My Lord you.
I never laughed, being bashful.
Lowering my head, I looked at the wall.
Called to, a thousand times, I never looked back.

At fifteen I stopped scowling,
I desired my dust to be mingled with yours
For ever and for ever and for ever.
Why should I climb the look out?

At sixteen you departed,
You went into far Ku-to-yen, by the river of swirling eddies,

And you have been gone five months.
The monkeys make sorrowful noise overhead.

You dragged your feet when you went out.
By the gate now, the moss is grown, the different mosses,
Too deep to clear them away!
The leaves fall early this autumn, in wind.
The paired butterflies are already yellow with August
Over the grass in the West garden;
They hurt me. I grow older.
If you are coming down through the narrows of the river Kiang,
Please let me know beforehand,
And I will come out to meet you
                         As far as Cho-fu-Sa.

Omar Kháyyám was an 11th-century Persian astronomer poet of Naishápur. His Rubáiyát in English translation was first published anonymously in 1859. Later Edward Fitzgerald acknowledged that he had translated the poem freely from the Persian. Fitzgerald, poet and translator, was a friend of Tennyson, Thackeray and Carlisle.

FROM THE RUBÁIYÁT OF OMAR KHÁYYÁM

Awake! for morning in the bowl of night
Has flung the stone that puts the stars to flight:
    And lo! the hunter of the East has caught
The Sultan's turret in a noose of light.

Come, fill the cup, and in the fire of spring
Your winter-garment of repentance fling;
    The bird of time has but a little way
To flutter – and the bird is on the wing.

Whether at Naishápur or Babylon,
Whether the cup with sweet or bitter run,
    The wine of life keeps oozing drop by drop,
The leaves of life keep falling one by one.

And look – a thousand blossoms with the day
Woke – and a thousand scatter'd into clay:
    And this first summer month that brings the rose
Shall take Jamshýd and Kaikobád away.

Well, let it take them! what have we to do
With Kaikobád the Great or Kaikhosrú?
    Let Zál and Rustum bluster as they will,
Or Hátim call to supper – heed not you.

With me along the strip of herbage strown
That just divides the desert from the sown,
    Where name of slave and sultan is forgot –
And peace to Mahmúd on his golden throne!

Here with a loaf of bread beneath the bough,
A flask of wine, a book of verse – and thou
    Beside me singing in the wilderness –
And wilderness is paradise enow!

For in and out, above, about, below,
'Tis nothing but a magic shadow-show
    Play'd in a box whose candle is the sun,
Round which we phantom figures come and go.

Hywel Ab Owain Gwynedd (12th century) Hywel was the illegitimate son of Prince Owain Gwynedd whose kingdom stretched from the river Dyfi to Chester. Only eight poems of Hywel are extant. I have adapted – very freely – one of his best poems. While boasting, he did not eschew the humour of self-mockery. Elsewhere, apart from boasting of his conquest of lovely women, he praised fulsomely the beauty of his native Wales and the bravery of its warriors. Soon after his father died in 1170, Hywel was killed in battle against two of his half-brothers.

BOAST POEM

Sunday, skilled in zealous verse I praise the Lord.
Monday, I sing in bed to my busty Nest,
'Such whiteness you are, pear blossom must be jealous.'
Tuesday, scholar Gwladus. Not to love her is a sin.
My couplets she pigeon-coos when I thrust to woo her
till her pale cheeks flush like rosy apple skin.
Wednesday, Generys. Dry old hymns I steal to please her.
Then with passion fruit in season I kneel to ease her.
Thursday, Hunydd, no hesitating lady, she.
One small cherry-englyn and she's my devotee.
Friday, worried Hawis, my epic regular.
She wants no baby, she's gooseberry vehement
till sugared by my poetry of endearment.
Saturday I score and score. One tidy eulogy
and I'm away – I can't brake – through an orchard
I adore. O sweet riot of efflorescence,
let her name be secret for her husband's sake,
my peach of a woman, my vegetarian diet.

O tongue, lick up the juices of the fruit. O teeth
– I've all of mine – be sure my busy tongue keeps quiet.

Christine de Pisan (1365–1430) was taken from her home in Venice to the French Court of Charles V as a young child. At the age of 15 she married a courtier, Etienne de Castel. In 1389 their happy marriage tragically ended when de Castel died in an epidemic, leaving his 25-year-old wife and three children. She had no inheritance but by writing about political life in Paris and the plight of women she admirably succeeded in supporting her family. Her lyrical poems are also of considerable quality. And she could be bitingly ironic.

IN PRAISE OF MARRIAGE

Marriage is a sweet state,
I can affirm it by my own experience,
In very truth, I who have a good and wise husband
Whom God helped me to find.
I give thanks to him who will save him for me,
For I can truly feel his great goodness
And for sure the sweet man loves me well.

Throughout that first night in our home,
I could well feel his great goodness,
For he did me no excess
That could hurt me.
But, before it was time to get up,
He kissed me 100 times, this I affirm,
Without exacting further outrage,
And yet for sure the sweet man loves me well.

He used to say to me in his soft language:
'God brought you to me,
Sweet lover, and I think he raised me
To be of use to you.'

And then he did not cease to dream
All night, his conduct was so perfect,
　Without seeking other excesses.
　And yet for sure the sweet man loves me well.

　O Princes, yet he drives me mad
　When he tells me he is all mine;
　He will destroy me with his gentle ways,
　And yet for sure the sweet man loves me well.

Sir Thomas Wyatt (1503–42) was a Member of Parliament and diplomat who translated Petrarch and became the first writer of sonnets in English. Wyatt held a number of important posts during the reign of Henry VIII. At one time he was suspected of being Anne Boleyn's lover and, as a consequence, was imprisoned. When ambassador in Spain he was accused of treason and again became a prisoner until he managed to clear his name. Some readers may be baffled by the word 'small' in the second verse of this famous poem. It was a synonym for 'slender' in the 16th century.

THEY FLEE FROM ME

They flee from me, that sometime did me seek
With naked foot stalking within my chamber.
Once have I seen them gentle tame and meek
That now are wild and do not once remember
That sometime they have put themselves in danger
To take bread at my hand; and now they range,
Busily seeking in continual change.

Thanked be fortune, it hath been otherwise
Twenty times better. But once especial,
In thin array, after a pleasant guise,
When her loose gown did from her shoulders fall,
And she me caught in her arms long and small,
And therewithal so sweetly did me kiss
And softly said, 'Dear heart, how like you this?'

It was no dream, for I lay broad awaking.
But all is turned now through my gentleness
Into a bitter fashion of forsaking.
And I have leave to go of her goodness,
And she also to use newfangledness.
But since that I unkindly so am served,
How like you this? What hath she now deserved?

Sir Philip Sidney (1554–86) was not only passionate about poetry but was also a man of action. At Court he became a favourite of Queen Elizabeth. When he was listed as a candidate for the crown of Poland, the Queen, afraid of 'losing the jewel of her time', prevented him from accepting the honour. As General of the Cavalry he was mortally wounded in battle against the Spaniards. England mourned him and his remains were brought to St Paul's in London for a public funeral.

MY TRUE LOVE HATH MY HEART

My true love hath my heart and I have his,
By just exchange one for the other given.
I hold his dear, and mine he cannot miss:
There never was a better bargain driven.
His heart in me keeps me and him in one;
My heart in him his thoughts and senses guides;
He loves my heart, for once it was his own;
I cherish his, because in me it bides.
His heart his wound received from my sight;
My heart was wounded with his wounded heart;
For as from me on him his hurt did light.
So still, methought, in me his hurt did smart;
    Both equal hurt, in this change sought our bliss:
    My true love hath my heart and I have his.

Anonymous 16th century

MY LOVE BOUND ME WITH A KISS

My Love bound me with a kiss
   That I should no longer stay;
When I felt so sweet a bliss
   I had less power to part away;
Alas! that women do not know
Kisses make men loath to go.

Yes, she knows it but too well,
   For I heard when Venus' dove
In her ear did softly tell
   That kisses were the seals of love;
O muse not then though it be so,
Kisses make men loath to go.

Wherefore did she thus inflame
   My desires, heat my blood
Instantly to quench the same
   And starve whom she had given food?
Ay, ay, the common sense can show
Kisses make men loath to go.

Had she bid me go at first
   It would ne'er have grieved my heart,
Hope delayed had been the worst;
   But ah to kiss and then to part!
How deep it struck, speak, gods, you know
Kisses make men loath to go.

Michael Drayton (1563–1631), the son of a Warwickshire butcher, being a studious and gifted boy, found rich and influential patrons who supported him through life. It is probable that he studied at Oxford. In 1626 he was styled 'Poet Laureate', but then that title implied no royal appointment. Indeed he paid court to King James but without success. After his death one of his aristocratic patrons erected a gold-inscribed monument to him in Westminster Abbey. The poem 'So well I love thee' was written the night before he died.

SINCE THERE'S NO HELP

Since there's no help, come, let us kiss and part.
Nay, I have done, you get no more of me;
And I am glad, yea, glad with all my heart,
That thus so cleanly I myself can free.
Shake hands for ever; cancel all our vows;
And when we meet at any time again,
Be it not seen in either of our brows
That we one jot of former love retain.
Now at the last gasp of Love's latest breath,
When, his pulse failing, Passion speechless lies,
When Faith is kneeling by his bed of death,
And Innocence is closing up his eyes;
Now, if thou would'st, when all have given him over,
From death to life thou might'st him yet recover.

SO WELL I LOVE THEE

So well I love thee as without thee I
Love nothing; if I might choose, I'd rather die
Than be one day debarred thy company.

Since beasts and plants do grow and live and move,
Beasts are those men that such a life approve:
He only lives that deadly is in love.

The corn, that in the ground is sown, first dies,
And of one seed do many ears arise;
Love, this world's corn, by dying multiplies.

The seeds of love first by thy eyes were thrown
Into a ground untilled, a heart unknown
To bear such fruit, till by thy hands 'twas sown.

Look as your looking-glass by chance may fall,
Divide and break in many pieces small,
And yet shows forth the self-same face in all,

Proportions, features, graces, just the same,
And in the smallest piece as well the name
Of fairest one deserves as in the richest frame;

So all my thoughts are pieces but of you,
Which put together make a glass so true
As I therein no other's face but yours can view.

Christopher Marlowe (1564–93), who was stabbed to death after a squalid quarrel at a dubious Deptford tavern, is known primarily for the poetry in his plays rather than for his poems. At the age of 23, soon after leaving Cambridge, he was amazing his contemporaries with his grand, rich tragedy, *Tamburlaine*. But, like Shakespeare, he could turn his genius to the writing of quieter love poems when moved to do so.

THE PASSIONATE SHEPHERD TO HIS LOVE

Come live with me and be my Love,
And we will all the pleasures prove
That hills and valleys, dale and field,
And all the craggy mountains yield.

There will we sit upon the rocks,
And see the shepherds feed their flocks,
By shallow rivers to whose falls
Melodious birds sing madrigals.

There will I make thee beds of roses
And a thousand fragrant posies,
A cap of flowers, and a kirtle
Embroidered all with leaves of myrtle.

A gown made of the finest wool
Which from our pretty lambs we pull;
Fair lined slippers for the cold,
With buckles of the purest gold.

A belt of straw and ivy buds,
With coral clasp and amber studs;
And if these pleasures may thee move,
Come live with me and be my Love.

Thy silver dishes for thy meat
As precious as the gods do eat,
Shall on an ivory table be
Prepared each day for thee and me.

The shepherd swains shall dance and sing
For thy delight each May morning:
If these delights thy mind may move,
Then live with me and be my Love.

William Shakespeare (1564–1616) During the last decade of the 16th century, sonnet writing became a fashionable pursuit. Shakespeare's sonnets were published in 1609, but were probably written during 1594 or 1595. Nobody is certain to whom they were addressed. Wordsworth said of the cycle that they unlocked Shakespeare's heart. Though many others have also assumed the sonnets to be autobiographical, it is possible the character depicted in them is as fictional as those in many of the plays. His first published poem was probably the long Ovidian narrative 'Venus and Adonis'. Shakespeare retells the sad, farcical, erotic story of unrequited love, of how the goddess Venus unsuccessfully woos the beautiful boy Adonis.

SONNET 29

When, in disgrace with Fortune and men's eyes,
I all alone beweep my outcast state,
And trouble deaf heaven with my bootless cries,
And look upon myself, and curse my fate,
Wishing me like to one more rich in hope,
Featur'd like him, like him with friends possess'd,
Desiring this man's art, and that man's scope,
With what I most enjoy contented least;
Yet in these thoughts myself almost despising,
Haply I think on thee, – and then my state,
Like to the lark at break of day arising
From sullen earth, sings hymns at heaven's gate;
 For thy sweet love remember'd such wealth brings,
 That then I scorn to change my state with kings.

SONNET 130

My mistress' eyes are nothing like the sun;
Coral is far more red than her lips' red:
If snow be white, why then her breasts are dun;
If hairs be wires, black wires grow on her head.
I have seen roses damask'd, red and white,
But no such roses see I in her cheeks;
And in some perfumes is there more delight
Than in the breath that from my mistress reeks.
I love to hear her speak, yet well I know
That music hath a far more pleasing sound:
I grant I never saw a goddess go;
My mistress, when she walks, treads on the ground.
  And yet, by heaven, I think my love as rare
  As any she belied with false compare.

FROM VENUS AND ADONIS

'Touch but my lips with those fair lips of thine –
Though mine be not so fair, yet are they red –
The kiss shall be thine own as well as mine.
What see'st thou in the ground? hold up thy head;
  Look in mine eyeballs, there thy beauty lies;
  Then why not lips on lips, since eyes in eyes?

'Art thou ashamed to kiss? then wink again,
And I will wink; so shall the day seem night.
Love keeps his revels where there are but twain;
Be bold to play, our sport is not in sight.
  These blue-veined violets whereon we lean
  Never can blab, nor know not what we mean.

'The tender spring upon thy tempting lip
Shews thee unripe; yet mayst thou well be tasted;
Make use of time, let not advantage slip;
Beauty within itself should not be wasted.
Fair flowers that are not gath'red in their prime
Rot and consume themselves in little time . . .'

Now gazeth she on him, now on the ground;
Sometime her arms infold him like a band;
She would, he will not in her arms be bound;
And when from thence he struggles to be gone,
She locks her lily fingers one in one.

'Fondling,' she saith, 'since I have hemmed thee here
Within the circuit of this ivory pale,
I'll be a park, and thou shalt be my deer;
Feed where thou wilt, on mountain or in dale;
Graze on my lips, and if those hills be dry,
Stray lower, where the pleasant fountains lie.

'Within this limit is relief enough,
Sweet bottom-grass and high delightful plain,
Round rising hillocks, brakes obscure and rough,
To shelter thee from tempest and from rain:
Then be my deer, since I am such a park;
No dog shall rouse thee, though a thousand bark.'

Thomas Campion (1567–1620) In middle age, Campion studied medicine at the University of Caen. But he was known as a poet and skilled musician who composed music for a number of his own lyrics. During the early years of James I's reign, he wrote a number of court masques. 'My Sweetest Lesbia' is an adaptation of a poem by the Latin poet Catullus 'Vivamus mea Lesbia, atque amemus'.

MY SWEETEST LESBIA

My sweetest Lesbia, let us live and love,
And though the sager sort our deeds reprove,
Let us not weigh them. Heaven's great lamps do dive
Into their west, and straight again revive;
But, soon as once set is our little light,
Then must we sleep one ever-during night.

If all would lead their lives in love like me,
Then bloody swords and armour should not be;
No drum nor trumpet peaceful sleeps should move,
Unless alarm came from the camp of love.
But fools do live and waste their little light,
And seek with pain their ever-during night.

When timely death my life and fortune ends,
Let not my hearse be vexed with mourning friends;
But let all lovers, rich in triumph, come
And with sweet pastimes grace my happy tomb:
And, Lesbia, close up thou my little light,
And crown with love my ever-during night.

John Donne (1573–1631) Ben Jonson called him 'The first poet in the world for some things.' Those 'some things' include his unsurpassed love poems and sonnets. In 1601 he clandestinely married Ann More, the niece of his employer, Sir Thomas Egerton, who promptly sacked him. For years Donne suffered economic hardship and was even jailed for a period before family reconciliation. He studied Divinity, Hebrew and Greek and, in 1610, took orders. In 1617 his wife died and Donne wrote little poetry afterwards, instead channelling his talents into the remarkable sermons he gave after becoming Dean of St Paul's in 1621.

THE GOOD MORROW

I wonder by my troth, what thou and I
    Did, till we loved? were we not weaned till then,
But sucked on country pleasures, childishly?
    Or snorted we in the seven sleepers' den?
'Twas so; but this, all pleasures fancies be,
If ever any beauty I did see,
Which I desired, and got, 'twas but a dream of thee.

And now good morrow to our waking souls,
    Which watch not one another out of fear;
For love, all love of other sights controls,
    And makes one little room, an everywhere.
Let sea-discoverers to new worlds have gone,
Let maps to others, worlds on worlds have shown,
Let us possess one world, each hath one, and is one.

My face in thine eye, thine in mine appears,
    And true plain hearts do in the faces rest;
Where can we find two better hemispheres
    Without sharp north, without declining west?
Whatever dies, was not mixed equally;

If our two loves be one, or, thou and I
Love so alike that none do slacken, none can die.

THE FLEA

Mark but this flea, and mark in this
How little that which thou deny'st me is;
Me it suck'd first, and now sucks thee,
And in this flea our two bloods mingled be;
Confess it: this cannot be said
A sin, or shame, or loss of maidenhead,
   Yet this enjoys before it woo,
    And pamper'd swells with one blood made of two,
    And this, alas, is more than we would do.

Oh stay, three lives in one flea spare,
Where we almost, nay more than married are:
This flea is you and I, and this
Our marriage bed, and marriage temple is;
Though parents grudge, and you, we're met
And cloister'd in these living walls of jet.
   Though use make you apt to kill me,
    Let not to that, self-murder added be,
    And sacrilege, three sins in killing three.

Cruel and sudden, hast thou since
Purpled thy nail in blood of innocence?
In what could this flea guilty be,
Except in that drop which it suck'd from thee?
Yet thou triumph'st, and say'st that thou
Find'st not thyself, nor me, the weaker now:
   'Tis true; then learn how false, fears be;
    Just so much honour, when thou yield'st to me,
    Will waste, as this flea's death took life from thee.

Robert Herrick (1591–1674) was the son of a wealthy goldsmith in Cheapside who committed suicide when the boy was barely a year old. Fortunately, Herrick had a rich uncle, also a goldsmith, who helped finance his education. Herrick was ordained in 1623 despite his youthful pagan tendencies and later became the clergyman in an isolated village, Dean Prior, in Devonshire. Most of his life he remained there, never marrying, surrounded by many domestic pets and writing love poems to the daughters of the country gentry. For a time he absconded from Devonshire with Tomasin Parsons, some 27 years younger than he and by whom he probably had an illegitimate daughter. He was a master of metre and charming, seemingly simple, love lyrics.

TO THE VIRGINS, TO MAKE MUCH OF TIME

Gather ye rosebuds while ye may,
    Old Time is still a-flying:
And this same flower that smiles today
    Tomorrow will be dying.

The glorious Lamp of Heaven, the Sun,
    The higher he's a-getting,
The sooner will his race be run
    And nearer he's to setting.

That age is best which is the first,
    When youth and blood are warmer;
But being spent, the worse, and worst
    Times still succeed the former.

Then be not coy, but use your time;
    And while ye may, go marry:
For having lost but once your prime,
    You may for ever tarry.

TO HIS MISTRESS OBJECTING TO HIM NEITHER TOYING OR TALKING

You say I love not, 'cause I do not play
Still with your curls, and kiss the time away.
You blame me too, because I can't devise
Some sport, to please those babies in your eyes;
By Love's religion, I must here confess it,
The most I love, when I the least express it.
Small griefs find tongues: Full casques are ever found
To give (if any, yet) but little sound.
Deep waters noiseless are; And this we know,
That chiding streams betray small depth below.
So when Love speechless is, she doth express
A depth in love, and that depth, bottomless.
Now since my love is tongue-less, know me such,
Who speak but little, 'cause I love so much.

Anne Bradstreet (1612–72) was born in Northampton, England, and educated privately, mainly in religious studies. In 1628 she married the Cambridge-educated Simon Bradstreet. Two years later they left for America and settled in Massachusetts. There, despite her busy family life – she bore eight children – she began to write poetry and prose. In 1650, without her knowledge, her poems were published in London. Partly because of the recent feminist movement and certainly because of her affecting later short poems, her reputation as the first American poet has been secured.

TO MY DEAR AND LOVING HUSBAND

If ever two were one, then surely we.
If ever man were loved by wife, then thee;
If ever wife was happy in a man,
Compare with me ye women if you can.
I prize thy love more than whole mines of gold,
Or all the riches that the East doth hold.
My love is such that rivers cannot quench,
Nor ought but love from thee, give recompense.
Thy love is such I can no way repay,
The heavens reward thee manifold I pray.
Then while we live, in love let's so persever,
That when we live no more, we may live ever.

BEFORE THE BIRTH OF ONE OF HER CHILDREN

All things within this fading world hath end,
Adversity doth still our joys attend;
No ties so strong, no friends so dear and sweet,
But with death's parting blow is sure to meet.
The sentence past is most irrevocable,
A common thing, yet oh, inevitable.
How soon, my Dear, death may my steps attend,
How soon't may be thy lot to lose thy friend.
We both are ignorant, yet love bids me
These farewell lines to recommend to thee,
That when that knot's untied that made us one,
I may seem thine, who in effect am none.
And if I see not half my days that's due,
What nature would, God grant to yours and you;
The many faults that well you know I have
Let be interred in my oblivious grave;
If any worth or virtue were in me,
Let that live freshly in thy memory
And when thou feel'st no grief, as I no harms,
Yet love thy dead, who long lay in thine arms.
And when thy loss shall be repaid with gains
Look to my little babes, my dear remains.
And if thou love thyself, or loved'st me,
These O protect from step-dame's injury.
And if chance to thine eyes shall bring this verse,
With some sad sighs honour my absent hearse;
And kiss this paper for thy love's dear sake,
Who with salt tears this last farewell did take.

Andrew Marvell (1621–78) No poet other than Marvell could boast of being an MP and a spy. He was elected to Parliament as Member for Hull in 1659. By this time he was already Oliver Cromwell's non-royal laureate. It is thought likely that while in Holland in 1662 he indulged in a little espionage for the British government. Marvell, friend of John Milton, was considered to be a patriot 'whom no bribe could buy and no flattery melt'. The wit and verve of his poetry is wonderfully displayed in this poem.

TO HIS COY MISTRESS

Had we but world enough, and time,
This coyness, Lady, were no crime.
We would sit down, and think which way
To walk, and pass our long love's day.
Thou by the Indian Ganges' side
Shouldst rubies find; I by the tide
Of Humber would complain. I would
Love you ten years before the Flood,
And you should, if you please, refuse
Till the conversion of the Jews.
My vegetable love should grow
Vaster than empires and more slow.
A hundred years should go to praise
Thine eyes, and on thy forehead gaze;
Two hundred to adore each breast,
But thirty thousand to the rest;
An age at least to every part,
And the last age should show your heart.
For, Lady, you deserve this state,
Nor would I love at a lower rate.
    But at my back I always hear
Time's winged chariot hurrying near;
  And yonder all before us lie
Deserts of vast eternity.

Thy beauty shall no more be found,
Nor, in thy marble vault, shall sound
My echoing song; then worms shall try
That long-preserved virginity,
And your quaint honour turn to dust,
And into ashes all my lust:
The grave's a fine and private place,
But none, I think, do there embrace.
    Now therefore, while the youthful hue
Sits on thy skin like morning dew,
And while thy willing soul transpires
At every pore with instant fires,
Now let us sport us while we may,
And now, like amorous birds of prey,
Rather at once our time devour
Than languish in his slow-chapped power.
Let us roll all our strength and all
Our sweetness up into one ball,
And tear our pleasures with rough strife
Through the iron gates of life;
Thus, though we cannot make our sun
Stand still, yet we will make him run.

Aphra Behn (1640–89) was born in Kent to an innkeeper. She married a city merchant of Dutch descent who died less than two years later. During the Dutch war she spied for Charles II. Thereafter she earned her living by writing plays, novels and poetry, the most successful play being **The Rover**. A visit she had paid to the British colony of Surinam before her marriage later inspired her most popular novel, **Oroonoko, or the History of the Royal Slave** in which she condemns the slave trade. Virginia Woolf wrote of her, 'All women together ought to let flowers fall on the tomb of Aphra Behn, which is, most scandalously but rather appropriately, in Westminster Abbey, for it was she who earned them the right to speak their minds.'

ON LOVING TWO EQUALLY

How strong does my passion flow,
Divided equally twixt two?
Damon had ne'er subdued my heart
Had not Alexis took his part;
Nor could Alexis powerful prove,
Without my Damon's aid, to gain my love.

When my Alexis present is,
Then I for Damon sigh and mourn;
But when Alexis I do miss,
Damon gains nothing but my scorn.
But if it chance that both are by,
For both alike I languish, sigh and die.

Cure then, thou mighty winged god,
This restless fever in my blood;
One-golden-pointed dart take back:

But which, O Cupid, will you take?
If Damon's, all my hopes are crossed;
Or that of my Alexis, I am lost.

John Wilmot, Earl of Rochester (1647–80) When eighteen years of age, the handsome and witty Rochester was presented to the court of 'the pleasure-loving monarch' Charles II. Soon he was to lead a wild life, having several mistresses even after he had married and fathered four children. Samuel Johnson reckoned that Rochester 'blazed out his youth in lavish voluptuousness'. Patron to a number of poets, not least John Dryden, Rochester himself wrote poetry that for its time was remarkably frank about sex. He died at the age of 32. Hollywood has not yet made a film of his life!

FROM THE PERFECT ENJOYMENT

Since now my Silvia is as kind as fair,
Let wit and joy succeed my dull despair.
Oh, what a night of pleasure was the last,
A full reward for all my troubles past!
And on my head if future mischief fall
This happy night shall make amends for all.
Nay, though my Silvia's love should turn to hate,
I'll think of this, and die contented with my fate.

Twelve was the lucky minute when we met
And on her bed were close together set;
Though listening spies might be perhaps too near,
Love filled our hearts, there was no room for fear.
Now whilst I strive her melting heart to move
With all the powerful eloquence of love,
In her fair cheeks I saw the colour rise
And an unusual softness in her eyes.
Gently they look, and I with joy adore
That only charm they never had before.
The wounds they made, her tongue was used to heal,
But now these gentle enemies reveal
A secret, which that friend would still conceal.

My eyes, transported too with amorous rage,
Seem fierce with expectation to engage;
But fast she holds my hands, and close her thighs,
And what she longs to do, with frowns denies:
A strange effect on foolish women wrought,
Bred in disguises, and by custom taught;
Custom, that prudence sometimes overrules,
But serves instead of reason to the fools!
Custom, which all the world to slavery brings,
The dull excuse for doing silly things!
She, by this method of her foolish sex,
Is forced awhile me and herself to vex.
But now, when thus we had been struggling long,
Her limbs grow weak, and her desires grow strong.
How can she hold to let the Hero in?
He storms without and Love betrays within.
Her hands at last, to hide her blushes, leave
The fort unguarded, willing to receive
My fierce assault, made with a lover's haste,
Like lightning piercing, and as quickly past.

Anonymous 17th century

FAIR HELEN

I wish I were where Helen lies;
Night and day on me she cries;
O that I were where Helen lies
   On fair Kirconnell lea!

Curst be the heart that thought the thought,
And curst the hand that fired the shot,
When in my arms burd Helen dropt,
   And died to succour me!

O think na but my heart was sair
When my Love dropt down and spak nae mair!
I laid her down wi' meikle care
   On fair Kirconnell lea.

As I went down the water-side,
None but my foe to be my guide,
None but my foe to be my guide,
   On fair Kirconnell lea;

I lighted down my sword to draw,
I hacked him in pieces sma',
I hacked him in pieces sma'
   For her sake that died for me.

O Helen fair, beyond compare!
I'll make a garland of thy hair
Shall bind my heart for evermair
   Until the day I die.

O that I were where Helen lies!
Night and day on me she cries;
    Out of my bed she bids me rise,
        Says, 'Haste and come to me!'

    O Helen fair! O Helen chaste!
    If I were with thee I were blest,
    Where thou lies low and takes thy rest
      On fair Kirconnell lea.

I wish my grave were growing green,
A winding-sheet drawn ower my een,
And I in Helen's arms lying,
    On fair Kirconnell lea.

I wish I were where Helen lies;
Night and day on me she cries;
And I am weary of the skies,
    Since my love died for me.

Robert Burns (1759–96), celebrated poet of Scotland, was the son of a struggling tenant farmer. Largely self-educated, Burns began writing verse while still a boy. His first book led to him being taken up by Edinburgh society. His immediate fame was perhaps partly responsible for this 'Heaven-taught' ploughman leading a life of libidinous excess and amorous entanglements. His radical views were at odds with the dour pieties of the age and his experience of inequality and poverty, along with his natural warmth and generosity of character, find expression in his musical poems whether written in the Scots dialect or in mainstream 18th-century English.

A RED, RED ROSE

O my luve is like a red, red rose
    That's newly sprung in June.
O my luve is like a melodie,
    That's sweetly played in tune.

As fair art thou, my bonnie lass,
    So deep in luve am I;
And I will luve thee still, my dear,
    Till a' the seas gang dry.

Till a' the seas gang dry, my dear,
    And the rocks melt wi' the sun;
And I will luve thee still, my dear,
    Till the sands o' life shall run.

And fair thee weel, my only luve,
    And fair thee weel a while!
And I will come again, my luve,
    Tho' it were ten thousand mile!

Lord Byron (1788–1824) It was said of this peer that after the publication of the first two Cantos of **Childe Harold** he awoke in London and found himself famous. Young, handsome, athletic – despite having a club foot – he was lionised in society at first until, through scandal, fame became infamy. In 1822, Shelley wrote in private correspondence that Byron 'touched the chord to which a million hearts responded and the coarse music which he produced to please them, disciplined him to the perfection to which he now approaches'. In 1823 Byron sailed to Greece to take part in the liberation of that country from Turkish rule. He died of a fever at Missolonghi, aged 36.

WHEN WE TWO PARTED

When we two parted
　In silence and tears,
Half broken-hearted
　To sever for years,
Pale grew thy cheek and cold,
　Colder thy kiss;
Truly that hour foretold
　Sorrow to this.

The dew of the morning
　Sunk chill on my brow –
It felt like the warning
　Of what I feel now.
Thy vows are all broken,
　And light is thy fame:
I hear thy name spoken,
　And share in its shame.

They name thee before me,
 A knell to mine ear;
A shudder comes o'er me –

 Why wert thou so dear?
They know not I knew thee,
 Who knew thee too well:–
Long, long shall I rue thee,
 Too deeply to tell.

In secret we met –
 In silence I grieve,
That thy heart could forget,
 Thy spirit deceive.
If I should meet thee
 After long years,
How should I greet thee?
 With silence and tears.

DONNA JULIA'S LETTER
(From Don Juan, Canto 1)

They tell me 'tis decided you depart:
    'Tis wise – 'tis well, but not the less a pain;
I have no further claim on your young heart,
    Mine is the victim, and would be again:
To love too much has been the only art
    I used; – I write in haste, and if a stain
Be on this sheet, 'tis not what it appears;
My eyeballs burn and throb, but have no tears.

I loved, I love you; for this love have lost
    State, station, heaven, mankind's, my own esteem,
And yet cannot regret what it hath cost,
    So dear is still the memory of that dream;
Yet, if I name my guilt, 'tis not to boast,
    None can deem harshlier of me than I deem:
I trace this scrawl because I cannot rest –
I've nothing to reproach or to request.

Man's love is of man's life a thing apart,
    'Tis woman's whole existence; man may range
The court, camp, church, the vessel, and the mart;
    Sword, gown, gain, glory, offer in exchange
Pride, fame, ambition, to fill up his heart,
    And few there are whom these cannot estrange;
Men have all these resources, we but one,
To love again, and be again undone.

You will proceed in pleasure, and in pride,
    Beloved and loving many; all is o'er
For me on earth, except some years to hide
    My shame and sorrow deep in my heart's core:
These I could bear, but cannot cast aside
    The passion which still rages as before, –
And so farewell – forgive me, love me – No,
That word is idle now – but let it go.

My breast has been all weakness, is so yet;
    But still I think I can collect my mind;
My blood still rushes where my spirit's set,
    As roll the waves before the settled wind;
My heart is feminine, nor can forget –
    To all, except one image, madly blind,
So shakes the needle, and so stands the pole,
As vibrates my fond heart to my fix'd soul.

I have no more to say, but linger still,
    And yet dare not set my seal upon this sheet,
And yet I may as well the task fulfil,
    My misery can scarce be more complete:
I had not lived till now, could sorrow kill;
    Death shuns the wretch who fain the blow would meet,
And I must even survive this last adieu,
And bear with life, to love and pray for you!

Percy Bysshe Shelley (1792–1822) was a hugely gifted Romantic poet, a rebel who believed in the perfectibility of mankind and who had a passion for reforming the world. Expelled from Oxford University for publishing a tract in favour of atheism, he was later termed 'a rare prodigy of crime and pollution'. Such opprobrium was not only due to his political activity and loathing of religion but also to his abandonment of his young wife who subsequently drowned herself. In 1818, Shelley, with his second wife, Mary, left England for Italy where he resided until drowning when his boat capsized in the Gulf of Spezzia.

LOVE'S PHILOSOPHY

The Fountains mingle with the River
    And the Rivers with the Ocean;
The winds of Heaven mix for ever
    With a sweet emotion;
Nothing in the world is single;
    All things by a law divine
In one another's being mingle,
    Why not I with thine? –

See the mountains kiss high Heaven
    And the waves clasp one another;
No sister-flower would be forgiven
    If it disdained its brother,
And the sunlight clasps the earth
    And the moonbeams kiss the sea:
What are all these kissings worth
    If thou kiss not me?

TO –

One word is too often profaned
   For me to profane it,
One feeling too falsely disdained
   For thee to disdain it.
One hope is too like despair
   For prudence to smother,
And pity from thee more dear
   Than that from another.

I can give not what men call love,
   But wilt thou accept not
The worship the heart lifts above
   And the Heavens reject not,
The desire of the moth for the star,
   Of the night for the morrow,
The devotion to something afar
   From the sphere of our sorrow?

John Clare (1793–1864) was born in Helpstone, Northamptonshire, the son of parish paupers. Clare, too, endured poverty throughout his life, working at times as a farm labourer or in the lime-pits at Ryall. He hoped to marry a neighbouring farmer's daughter, Mary Joyce, but her father would not allow it. In 1820 he published his first book of verse in which he described country scenery and rustic events. That year he married Martha 'Patty' Turner, though still in love with Mary. Always of a nervous disposition, his mental health deteriorated until eventually he was certified insane. During his time at Northampton General Asylum, Clare wrote some of his most poignant poems.

FIRST LOVE

I ne'er was struck before that hour
    With love so sudden and so sweet,
Her face it bloomed like a sweet flower
    And stole my heart away complete.
My face turned pale as deadly pale,
    My legs refused to walk away,
And when she looked, what could I ail?
    My life and all seemed turned to clay.

And then my blood rushed to my face
    And took my eyesight quite away,
The trees and bushes round the place
    Seemed midnight at noonday.
I could not see a single thing,
    Words from my eyes did start –
They spoke as chords do from the string,
    And blood burnt round my heart.

Are flowers the winter's choice?
   Is love's bed always snow?

She seemed to hear my silent voice,
   Not love's appeals to know.
I never saw so sweet a face
   As that I stood before.
My heart has left its dwelling-place
   And can return no more.

MARRIED TO A SOLDIER

The pride of all the village,
   The fairest to be seen,
The pride of all the village
   That might have been a queen,
Has bid goodbye to neighbours
   And left the dance and play
And married to a soldier
   And wandered far away.

The cottage is neglected,
   Where young men used to go
And talk about her beauty
   And see her come and go;
The bench agen her cottage
   Where she used to work at eve
Is vanished with the woodbine;
   And all are taken leave.

Her cottage is neglected,
    Her garden gathers green,
The summer comes unnoticed,
    Her flowers are never seen;
There's none to tie a blossom up
    Or clean a weed away;
She's married to a soldier
    And wandered far away.

The neighbours wonder at her,
    And surely well they may,
To think one so could flatter
    Her heart to go away.
But the cocked hat and the feather
    Appeared so very gay,
She bundled clothes together
    And married far away.

John Keats (1795–1821), when dying of tuberculosis, asked his friend, Joseph Severn, that his gravestone should bear the words, 'Here lies one whose name was writ in water'. But his name is known and will be known as long as English poetry is read. Keats began writing in 1813 and continued to do so while studying medicine at Guy's Hospital in London. Keats's inordinately pronounced identification with suffering patients resulted in him giving up the practice of medicine soon after he qualified. The sonnet included here was written on a blank page in his copy of Shakespeare's poems, facing 'A Lover's Complaint', as he sailed to Italy; he later died in Rome. No doubt Keats had in mind his thwarted love for Fanny Brawne when he wrote it.

LAST SONNET

Bright star! would I were steadfast as thou art –
  Not in lone splendour hung aloft the night,
And watching, with eternal lids apart,
  Like Nature's patient, sleepless Eremite,
The moving waters at their priestlike task
  Of pure ablution round earth's human shores,
Or gazing on the new soft-fallen mask
  Of snow upon the mountains and the moors –
No – yet still steadfast, still unchangeable,
  Pillowed upon my fair love's ripening breast,
To feel for ever its soft fall and swell,
  Awake for ever in a sweet unrest,
Still, still to hear her tender-taken breath,
And so live ever – or else swoon to death.

LA BELLE DAME
SANS MERCI

O what can ail thee, knight-at-arms,
   Alone and palely loitering?
The sedge has withered from the lake,
   And no birds sing.

O, what can ail thee, knight-at-arms,
   So haggard and so woe-begone?
The squirrel's granary is full
   And the harvest's done.

I see a lily on thy brow
   With anguish moist and fever dew,
And on thy cheeks a fading rose
   Fast withereth too.

I met a lady in the meads,
   Full beautiful – a faery's child,
Her hair was long, her foot was light,
   And her eyes were wild.

I made a garland for her head,
   And bracelets too, and fragrant zone;
She looked at me as she did love,
   And made sweet moan.

I set her on my pacing steed,
   And nothing else saw all day long,
For sidelong would she bend, and sing
   A faery's song.

She found me roots of relish sweet,
   And honey wild, and manna dew
And sure in language strange she said –
   'I love thee true'.

She took me to her elfin grot,
  And there she wept, and sighed full sore,
And there I shut her wild wild eyes
  With kisses four.

And there she lulled me asleep,
  And there I dreamed – Ah! woe betide!
The latest dream I ever dreamed
  On the cold hill's side.

I saw pale kings and princes too,
  Pale warriors, death-pale were they all;
They cried – 'La Belle Dame sans Merci
  Hath thee in thrall!'

I saw their starved lips in the gloam,
  With horrid warning gaped wide,
And I awoke and found me here,
  On the cold hill's side.

And this is why I sojourn here,
  Alone and palely loitering,
Though the sedge is withered from the lake,
  And no birds sing.

Heinrich Heine (1797–1856) was the son of Jewish parents who called him by the rather less Germanic name of Harry. Having been born in Dusseldorf, however, Heine thought of himself as a true Rhinelander. In a letter of 1824, he wrote, that what water was to the fish, German-ness was to him. After 1830, because of German anti-semitism, he settled in Paris, supporting himself by his literary endeavours and writing in both French and German. He became famous for his biting wit, irony and masterly lyrics.

A WOMAN

Each loved the other beyond belief;
She lived by her wits and he was a thief.
He played the Fool and fooled the crowd;
She sprawled on the bed and laughed aloud.

The days ticked by with joy and with jest;
At night she swooned upon his breast.
When the policeman came, the skies all cloud,
She thought it funny and laughed aloud.

He sent her a letter, 'Oh come to me,
By day and by night I long for thee.
Love is forever, that's what we vowed.'
She shook her head and laughed aloud.

At six in the morning they hung him high
– For fooling and thieving he had to die.
At seven o'clock he lay stiff in his shroud;
And she quaffed red wine and laughed aloud.

Adaptation by Dannie Abse

Elizabeth Barrett Browning (1806–61) had a larger public following than her husband, Robert, during her lifetime. She was always of a nervous and delicate constitution and spent many years in her father's house at London's Wimpole Street in the seclusion of an invalid's room. Her 'Sonnets from the Portuguese' were composed during the period Robert was courting her. Despite Elizabeth's authoritative father who would not sanction their marriage, they wed secretly and settled in Italy, mainly in Florence.

FROM SONNETS FROM THE PORTUGUESE

How do I love thee? Let me count the ways.
I love thee to the depth and breadth and height
My soul can reach, when feeling out of sight
For the ends of Being and ideal Grace.
I love thee to the level of everyday's
Most quiet need, by sun and candle-light.
I love thee freely, as men strive for Right;
I love thee purely, as they turn from Praise.
I love thee with the passion put to use
In my old griefs, and with my childhood's faith.
I love thee with a love I seemed to lose
With my lost saints, – I love thee with the breath,
Smiles, tears, of all my life! – and if God choose,
I shall but love thee better after death.

Alfred, Lord Tennyson (1809–92) was born of a Lincolnshire family that the poet said 'had black blood in it' and was physically a swarthy gypsy of a man. When eight years old, he imitated the verse of every poet he read. Tennyson once spoke of his mastery of the English language only to add, 'But I have nothing to say.' His lyrics are so melodious and so exquisitely coloured that a reader may well ask, 'Does a jewel need to have a significant philosophy?' His first heterogeneous long poem, 'The Princess', where lyrics – like pearls – thread through the story, was first published in 1847.

FROM THE PRINCESS

Come down, O maid, from yonder mountain height:
What pleasure lives in height (the Shepherd sang)
In height and cold, the splendour of the hills?
But cease to move so near the Heavens, and cease
To glide a sunbeam by the blasted Pine,
To sit a star upon the sparkling spire;
And come, for Love is of the valley, come,
For Love is of the valley, come thou down
And find him; by the happy threshold, he,
Or hand in hand with Plenty in the maize,
Or red with spirted purple of the vats,
Or foxlike in the vine; nor cares to walk
With Death and Morning on the silver horns,
Nor wilt thou snare him in the white ravine,
Nor find him dropt upon the firths of ice,
That huddling slant in furrow-cloven falls
To roll the torrent out of dusky doors:
But follow: let the torrent dance thee down
To find him in the valley; let the wild
Lean-headed Eagles yelp alone, and leave
The monstrous ledges there to slope, and spill
Their thousand wreaths of dangling water-smoke,
    That like a broken purpose waste in air:

So waste not thou; but come; for all the vales
Await thee; azure pillars of the hearth
Arise to thee; the children call, and I
Thy shepherd pipe, and sweet is every sound,
Sweeter thy voice, but every sound is sweet;
Myriads of rivulets hurrying thro' the lawn,
The moan of doves in immemorial elms,
And murmuring of innumerable bees.

Now sleeps the crimson petal, now the white;
Nor waves the cypress in the palace walk;
Nor winks the gold fin in the porphyry font:
The firefly wakens: waken thou with me.

Now droops the milkwhite peacock like a ghost,
And like a ghost she glimmers on to me.

Now lies the earth all Danae to the stars,
And all thy heart lies open unto me.

Now slides the silent meteor on, and leaves
A shining furrow, as thy thoughts in me.

Now folds the lily all her sweetness up,
And slips into the bosom of the lake:
So fold thyself, my dearest, thou, and slip
Into my bosom and be lost in me.

As thro' the land at eve we went
    And pluck'd the ripen'd ears,
We fell out, my wife and I,
O we fell out, I know not why,
    And kiss'd again with tears.

And blessings on the falling out
   That all the more endears,
When we fall out with those we love,
   And kiss again with tears.

For when we came where lies the child
   We lost in other years,
There above the little grave
O there above the little grave,
   We kiss'd again with tears.

Robert Browning (1812–89) is in some ways, along with Walt Whitman, the father of modern poetry. During his early years, like others, he had to endure critical derision. Recognition came later in life. In 1881 a Browning Society was formed to study his muscular, humorous, lyrical and dramatic works. His sense of character was wonderfully fine as is witnessed by his persona poems where he makes his imagined characters speak. His best love poems were written between 1845, when he first met his future wife, and 1861, when she died. He survived Elizabeth for 28 years.

A WOMAN'S LAST WORD

Let's contend no more, Love,
    Strive nor weep:
All be as before, Love,
    – Only sleep!

What so wild as words are?
    I and thou
In debate, as birds are,
    Hawk on Bough!

See the creature stalking
    While we speak!
Hush and hide the talking,
    Cheek on cheek!

What so false as truth is,
    False to thee?
Where the serpent's tooth is,
    Shun the tree –

Where the apple reddens
  Never pry –
Lest we lose our Edens,
  Eve and I!

Be a god and hold me
  With a charm!
Be a man and fold me
  With thine arm!

Teach me, only teach, Love!
  As I ought
I will speak thy speech, Love,
  Think thy thought –

Meet, if thou require it,
  Both demands,
Laying flesh and spirit
  In thy hands.

That shall be tomorrow
  Not tonight:
I must bury sorrow
  Out of sight:

– Must a little weep, Love,
  (Foolish me!)
And so fall asleep, Love
  Loved by thee.

A LIGHT WOMAN

So far as our story approaches the end,
　　Which do you pity the most of us three? –
My friend, or the mistress of my friend
　　With her wanton eyes, or me?

My friend was already too good to lose,
　　And seemed in the way of improvement yet,
When she crossed his path with her hunting-noose
　　And over him drew her net.

When I saw him tangled in her toils,
　　A shame, said I, if she adds just him
To her nine-and-ninety other spoils,
　　The hundredth, for a whim!

And before my friend be wholly hers,
　　How easy to prove to him, I said
An eagle's the game her pride prefers,
　　Though she snaps at the wren instead!

So, I gave her eyes my own eyes to take,
　　My hand sought hers as in earnest need,
And round she turned for my noble sake,
　　And gave me herself indeed.

The eagle am I, with my fame in the world,
　　The wren is he, with his maiden face.
– You look away and your lip is curled?
　　Patience, a moment's space!

For see – my friend goes shaking and white;
　　He eyes me as the basilisk:
I have turned, it appears, his day to night,
　　Eclipsing his sun's disk.

And I did it, he thinks, as a very thief:
　　'Though I love her – that he comprehends –
One should master one's passions, (love in chief)
　　And be loyal to one's friends!'

And she – she lies in my hand as tame
　　As a pear late basking over a wall;
Just a touch to try and off it came;
　　'Tis mine – can I let it fall?

With no mind to eat it, that's the worst!
　　Were it thrown in the road, would the case assist?
'Twas quenching a dozen blue-flies' thirst
　　When I gave its stalk a twist.

And I, – what I seem to my friend, you see –
　　What I soon shall seem to his love, you guess.
What I seem to myself, do you ask of me?
　　No hero, I confess.

'Tis an awkward thing to play with souls,
　　And matter enough to save one's own.
Yet think of my friend, and the burning coals
　　He played with for bits of stone!

One likes to show the truth for the truth;
　　That the woman was light is very true:
But suppose she says, – Never mind that youth!
　　What wrong have I done to you?

Well, any how, here the story stays,
　　So far at least as I understand;
And, Robert Browning, you writer of plays,
　　Here's a subject made to your hand!

Emily Brontë (1818–48) lived in the parsonage at Haworth, near Bradford, all of her life except for a short period when she was a governess in Halifax. She and her sisters, Charlotte and Anne, wrote poems and prose under masculine pseudonyms, hers being Ellis Bell. She was the most gifted poet of the sisters but her most famous work was the novel **Wuthering Heights**, which was published in 1847, a year before her death from tuberculosis.

REMEMBRANCE

Cold in the earth – and the deep snow piled above thee,
Far, far removed, cold in the dreary grave!
Have I forgot, my only Love, to love thee,
Severed at last by Time's all-severing wave?

Now, when alone, do my thoughts no longer hover
Over the mountains, on that northern shore,
Resting their wings where heath and fern-leaves cover
Thy noble heart for ever, ever more?

Cold in the earth – and fifteen wild Decembers
From those brown hills have melted into spring –
Faithful indeed is the spirit that remembers
After such years of change and suffering!

Sweet love of youth, forgive if I forget thee
While the world's tide is bearing me along:
Other desires and other hopes beset me,
Hopes which obscure, but cannot do thee wrong!

No later light has lightened up my heaven;
No second morn has ever shone for me:
All my life's bliss from thy dear life was given –
All my life's bliss is in the grave with thee.

But, when the days of golden dreams had perished,
And even Despair was powerless to destroy,
Then did I learn how existence should be cherished,
Strengthened, and fed without the aid of joy;

Then did I check the tears of useless passion,
Weaned my young soul from yearning after thine;
Sternly denied its burning wish to hasten
Down to that tomb already more than mine!

And, even yet, I dare not let it languish
Dare not indulge in Memory's rapturous pain;
Once drinking deep of that divinest anguish,
How could I seek the empty world again?

Dante Gabriel Rossetti (1828–82), poet and painter, was born in London, the son of a Neapolitan refugee. He was a leading member of the Pre-Raphaelite school and a number of his sonnets refer to works of art. He married his model, Elizabeth Siddal, and when she killed herself in 1862, grief-stricken, he buried his poetry manuscripts in her grave. He exhumed these in 1869 when he published his first book of poems. It has been said of his poems that they 'expressed passion of wedded love in rapture and desolation'.

SUDDEN LIGHT

I have been here before,
But when or how I cannot tell:
I know the grass beyond the door,
The sweet keen smell,
The sighing sound, the lights around the shore.

You have been mine before, –
How long ago I may not know:
But just when at that swallow's soar
Your neck turned so,
Some veil did fall – I knew it all of yore.

Then, now, – perchance again! . . .
O round mine eyes your tresses shake!
Shall we not lie as we have lain
Thus for Love's sake,
And sleep, and wake, yet never break the chain?

Christina Rossetti (1830–94) was the younger of Dante Gabriel Rossetti's sisters and the only woman member of the Pre-Raphaelite company. Like her mother she was a devout Anglican and rejected, though not without much heart-searching, two suitors on religious grounds. Her High Anglican piety led her to break off her engagement to a Pre-Raphaelite painter, James Collinson, when he became a Roman Catholic. Living in London, she devoted attention to her mother and aunts in their old age and to service of the church. Because so much of her poetry was preoccupied with death Alice Meynell said, 'Her portrait should have been painted with the skull on the table. Her most admirable poems are fresh and poignant and possess sure musical resonance.'

LOVE FROM THE NORTH

I had a love in soft south land,
    Beloved through April far in May;
He waited on my lightest breath,
    And never dared to say me nay.

He saddened if my cheer was sad,
    But gay he grew if I was gay;
We never differed on a hair,
    My yes his yes, my nay his nay.

The wedding hour was come, the aisles
    Were flushed with sun and flowers that day;
I pacing balanced in my thoughts:
    'It's quite too late to think of nay'. –

My bridegroom answered in his turn,
    Myself had almost answered 'yea':
When through the flashing nave I heard
    A struggle and resounding 'nay'.

Bridemaids and bridegroom shrank in fear,
  But I stood high who stood at bay:
'And if I answer yea, fair Sir,
What man art thou to bar with nay?'

He was a strong man from the north,
  Light-locked, with eyes of dangerous gray:
'Put yea by for another time
In which I will not say thee nay.'

He took me in his strong white arms,
  He bore me on his horse away
O'er crag, morass, and hairbreadth pass,
  But never asked me yea or nay.

He made me fast with book and bell,
  With links of love he makes me stay;
Till now I've neither heart nor power
  Nor will nor wish to say him nay.

SONNET

I wish I could remember that first day,
First hour, first moment of your meeting me,
If bright or dim the season, it might be
Summer or Winter for aught I can say;
So unrecorded did it slip away,
So blind was I to see and foresee,
So dull to mark the budding of my tree
That would not blossom yet for many a May.
If only I could recollect it, such
A day of days! I let it come and go
As traceless as a thaw of byegone snow:

It seemed to mean so little, meant so much;
If only now I could recall that touch,
First touch of hand in hand – Did one but know!

Thomas Hardy (1840–1928) poet and novelist, the son of a Dorset stonemason, was trained as an architect. But his pressing need was to write – novels and poetry. He was about twenty years old when he began writing verse but his first book, **Wessex Poems**, did not appear until 1898 after he had written several successful novels. During the last years of his life he produced volume after volume of shorter poems – 'lyrical, narrative and reflective'. So prolific was he that his posthumous **Collected Poems** contained more than 900 poems. Among the most personal and poignant poems that he wrote were elegies recollecting his first wife, Emma, who died in 1912.

THE VOICE

Woman much missed, how you call to me, call to me,
Saying that now you are not as you were
When you had changed from the one who was all to me,
But as at first, when our day was fair.

Can it be you that I hear? Let me view you, then,
Standing as when I drew near to the town
Where you would wait for me: yes, as I knew you then,
Even to the original air-blue gown!

Or is it only the breeze, in its listlessness
Travelling across the wet mead to me here,
You being ever dissolved to wan wistlessness,
Heard no more again far or near?

   Thus I; faltering forward,
   Leaves around me falling,
Wind oozing thin through the thorn from norward
   And the woman calling.

December 1912

AFTER A JOURNEY

Hereto I come to view a voiceless ghost;
    Whither, O whither will its whim now draw me?
Up the cliff, down, till I'm lonely, lost,
    And the unseen waters' ejaculations awe me.
Where you will next be there's no knowing,
    Facing round about me everywhere,
      With your nut-coloured hair,
And grey eyes, and rose-flush coming and going.

Yes: I have re-entered your olden haunts at last;
    Through the years, through the dead scenes I have tracked
      you;
What have you now found to say of our past –
    Scanned across the dark space wherein I have lacked you?
Summer gave us sweets, but autumn wrought division?
    Things were not lastly as firstly well
      With us twain, you tell?
But all's closed now, despite Time's derision.

I see what you are doing: you are leading me on
    To the spots we knew when we haunted here together,
The waterfall, above which the mist-bow shone
    At the then fair hour in the then fair weather,
And the cave just under, with a voice still so hollow
    That it seems to call out to me from forty years ago,
      When you were all aglow,
And not the thin ghost that I now fraily follow!

Ignorant of what there is flitting here to see,
   The waked birds preen and the seals flop lazily,
Soon you will have, Dear, to vanish from me,
   For the stars close their shutters and the dawn whitens
     hazily.

Trust me, I mind not, though Life lours,
   The bringing me here; nay, bring me here again!
    I am just the same as when
Our days were a joy, and our path through flowers.

                    Pentargan Bay.

Anonymous 19th century

FRANKIE AND JOHNNY

Frankie and Johnny were lovers,
    Lordy, how they could love,
Swore to be true to each other,
    True as the stars up above,
        He was her man, but he done her wrong.

Frankie went down to the corner,
    To buy her a bucket of beer,
Frankie says 'Mister Bartender,
    Has my lovin' Johnny been here?
        He is my man, but he's doing me wrong.'

'I don't want to cause you no trouble
    Don't want to tell you no lie,
I saw your Johnny half-an-hour ago
    Making love to Nelly Bly,
        He is your man, but he's doing you wrong.'

Frankie went down to the hotel
    Looked over the transom so high,
There she saw her lovin' Johnny
    Making love to Nelly Bly.
        He was her man; he was doing her wrong.

Frankie threw back her kimono,
    Pulled out her big forty-four;
Rooty-toot-toot three times she shot
    Right through that hotel door.
        She shot her man, who was doing her wrong.

'Roll me over gently,
   Roll me over slow,
Roll me over on my right side,
   'Cause these bullets hurt me so,
      I was your man, but I done you wrong.'

Bring all your rubber-tyred hearses
   Bring all your rubber-tyred hacks,
They're carrying poor Johnny to the burying ground
   And they ain't gonna bring him back,
      He was her man, but he done her wrong.

Frankie says to the sheriff,
   'What are they going to do?'
The sheriff he said to Frankie,
   'It's the 'lectric chair for you.
      He was your man, and he done you wrong.'

'Put me in that dungeon,
   Put me in that cell,
Put me where the northeast wind
   Blows from the southeast corner of hell,
      I shot my man, 'cause he done me wrong.'

Charlotte Mew (1869–1928) was born in Bloomsbury, the daughter of a London architect. When her father died – she was then 29 years old – she became a teacher and lived with her mother and sister in genteel poverty. Her first book of poems, *The Farmer's Bride*, appeared when she was 47; her second volume, *The Rambling Sailor,* was published posthumously in 1929. Thomas Hardy and Virginia Woolf called her the greatest living woman poet. There had always been a history of mental instability in her family and, after her mother and sister died, Charlotte Mew took her life by drinking disinfectant while in a nursing home.

THE FARMER'S BRIDE

Three summers since I chose a maid,
Too young may be – but more's to do
At harvest-time than bide and woo.
    When us was wed she turned afraid
Of love and me and all things human;
Like the shut of a winter's day
Her smile went out, and 'twasn't a woman –
    More like a little frightened fay.
        One night, in the Fall, she runned away.

'Out 'mong the sheep, her be,' they said.
Should properly have been abed;
    But sure enough she wadn't there
    Lying awake with her wide brown stare.
Over seven-acre field and up-along across the down
    We chased her, flying like a hare
    Before our lanterns. To Church-Town
        All in a shiver and a scare
    We caught her, fetched her home at last
        And turned the key upon her, fast.

She does the work about the house
As well as most, but like a mouse:
    Happy enough to chat and play
    With birds and rabbits and such as they,
    So long as men-folk keep away.
'Not near, not near!' her eyes beseech
When one of us comes within reach.
    The women say that beasts in stall
    Look round like children at her call.
    I've hardly heard her speak at all.

Shy as a leveret, swift as he,
Straight and slight as a young larch tree,
Sweet as the first wild violets, she,
To her wild self. But what to me?
The short days shorten and the oaks are brown,
    The blue smoke rises to the low grey sky.
One leaf in the still air falls slowly down,
    A magpie's spotted feathers lie
On the black earth spread white with rime,
The berries redden up to Christmas-time.
    What's Christmas-time without there be
    Some other in the house than we!

    She sleeps up in the attic there
    Alone, poor maid. 'Tis but a stair
    Betwixt us. Oh! my God! the down,
    The soft young down of her, the brown,
The brown of her – her eyes, her hair, her hair!

Edward Thomas (1878–1917) married Helen Noble while she was still a student at Oxford and decided to make a living by writing. Though he wrote 30 books of poetic prose he and his family lived a life of economic hardship. Persuaded by his friend, Robert Frost, he began writing poetry at the age of 37. Over the next two years he wrote more than one hundred poems. His first collection, published under the pseudonym Edward Eastaway, appeared soon after he was killed in the trenches at Arras in 1917. A further volume was published, under his own name, the following year. Thomas's accessible, moving and pleasurable poetry was overlooked for many years.

AND YOU, HELEN

And you, Helen, what should I give you?
So many things I would give you
Had I an infinite great store
Offered me and I stood before
To choose. I would give you youth,
All kinds of loveliness and truth,
A clear eye as good as mine,
Lands, waters, flowers, wine,
As many children as your heart
Might wish for, a far better art
Than mine can be, all you have lost,
Upon the travelling waters tossed,
Or given to me. If I could choose
Freely in that great treasure-house
Anything from any shelf,
I would give you back yourself,
And power to discriminate
What you want and want it not too late,
Many fair days free from care
And heart to enjoy both foul and fair,
And myself, too, if I could find
Where it lay hidden and it proved kind.

NO ONE SO MUCH AS YOU

No one so much as you
Loves this my clay,
Or would lament as you
Its dying day.

You know me through and through
Though I have not told,
And though with what you know
You are not bold.

None ever was so fair
As I thought you:
Not a word can I bear
Spoken against you.

All that I ever did
For you seemed coarse
Compared with what I hid
Nor put in force.

My eyes scarce dare meet you
Lest they should prove
I but respond to you
And do not love.

We look and understand,
We cannot speak
Except in trifles and
Words most weak.

For I at most accept
Your love, regretting
That is all: I have kept
Only a fretting

That I could not return
All that you gave
And could not ever burn
With the love you have,

Till sometimes it did seem
Better it were
Never to see you more
Than linger here

With only gratitude
Instead of love –
A pine in solitude
Cradling a dove.

D H Lawrence (1885–1930) 'If you don't like your work, don't do it,' advised Lawrence, the son of a Nottingham miner in a mother-dominated family. And so Lawrence gave up being a schoolmaster to become a full-time author. He began writing poems when he was nineteen years old and his best verse may well outlast his celebrated novels. His poetry, like his fiction, is often thinly disguised autobiography. Throughout his writing life Lawrence tried to plumb the depths of the elemental origins of his being and 'to think with the blood'. As Aldous Huxley aptly wrote, after Lawrence had died of tuberculosis, 'He was always intensely aware of the mystery of the world, and the mystery was always to him a *numen*, divine.'

SHE SAID AS WELL TO ME

She said as well to me: 'Why are you ashamed?
That little bit of your chest that shows between
the gap of your shirt, why cover it up?
Why shouldn't your legs and your good strong thighs
be rough and hairy? – I'm glad they are like that.
You are shy, you silly, you silly shy thing.
Men are the shyest creatures, they never will come
out of their covers. Like any snake
slipping into its bed of dead leaves, you hurry into your clothes.
And I love you so! Straight and clean and all of a piece is the
    body of a man,
such an instrument, a spade, like a spear, or an oar,
such a joy to me –'
So she laid her hands and pressed them down my sides,
so that I began to wonder over myself, and what I was.

She said to me: 'What an instrument your body!
single and perfectly distinct from everything else!
What a tool in the hands of the Lord!
Only God could have brought it to its shape.
It feels as if his handgrasp, wearing you
had polished you and hollowed you,
hollowed this groove in your sides, grasped you under the
    breasts
and brought you to the very quick of your form,
subtler than an old, soft-worn fiddle-bow.

'When I was a child, I loved my father's riding-whip
that he used so often.
I loved to handle it, it seemed like a near part of him.
So I did his pens, and the jasper seal on his desk.
Something seemed to surge through me when I touched them.

'So it is with you, but here
The joy I feel!
God knows what I feel, but it is joy!
Look, you are clean and fine and singled out!
I admire you so, you are so beautiful: this clean sweep of
    your sides, this firmness, this hard mould!
I would die rather than have it injured with one scar.
I wish I could grip you like the fist of the Lord,
and have you –'

So she said, and I wondered,
feeling trammelled and hurt.
It did not make me free.

Now I say to her: 'No tool, no instrument, no God!
Don't touch me and appreciate me.
It is an infamy.
You would think twice before you touched a weasel on a fence
as it lifts its straight white throat.
Your hand would not be so flig and easy.
Nor the adder we saw asleep with her head on her shoulder,
curled up in the sunshine like a princess;
when she lifted her head in delicate, startled wonder
you did not stretch forward to caress her
though she looked rarely beautiful
and a miracle as she glided delicately away, with such dignity.
And the young bull in the field, with his wrinkled, sad face,
you are afraid if he rises to his feet,
though he is all wistful and pathetic, like a monolith,
    arrested, static.

'Is there nothing in me to make you hesitate?
I tell you there is all these,
And why should you overlook them in me? –'

Marina Tsvetaeva (1892–1941) was the Moscow-born daughter of a Professor of Art and a concert pianist of Polish-German lineage. She began writing verse early and two of her books were published when she was still in her teens. Tsvetaeva reacted strongly against the Revolution as did her husband who fought for the Whites. In 1922 she left Soviet Russia to live in exile. Her autobiographical poetry reflects her nostalgia for Russia and her romantic emotional entanglements. During her last years in Paris, when her husband was too ill to work, she experienced extreme poverty and felt despairingly isolated as a person and neglected as a poet.

AN ATTEMPT AT
JEALOUSY

How is your life with the other one,
    simpler, isn't it? One   stroke of the oar
then a long coastline, and soon
    even the memory of me

will be a floating island
    (in the sky, not on the waters):
spirits, spirits, you will be
    sisters, and never lovers.

How is your life with an ordinary
    woman?   without godhead?
Now that your sovereign has
    been deposed (and you have stepped down).

How is your life? Are you fussing?
    flinching? How   do you get up?
The tax of deathless vulgarity
    can you cope with it, poor man?

'Scenes and hysterics   I've had
    enough! I'll rent my own house.'
  How is your life with the other one
      now, you that I chose for my own?

More to your taste, more delicious
    is it, your food? Don't moan if you sicken.
  How is your life with an *image*
      you, who walked on Sinai?

How is your life with a stranger
    from this world? Can you (be frank)
  love her? Or do you   feel shame
      like Zeus's reins on your forehead?

How is your life? Are you
    healthy? How do you   sing?
  How do you deal with the pain
      of an undying conscience, poor man?

How is your life with a piece of market
    stuff, at a steep price?
  After Carrara marble,
      how is your life with the dust of

plaster now? (God was hewn from
    stone, but he is smashed to bits.)
  How do you live with one of a
      thousand women   after Lilith?

Sated with newness, are you?
    Now you are grown cold to magic,
  how is your life with an
      earthly woman, without a sixth

sense? Tell me: are you happy?
Not? In a shallow pit? How is
your life, my love? Is it as
hard as mine with another man?

Translated by Elaine Feinstein

Robert Graves (1895–1985) the son of an 'Irish man of Letters' and a German mother, began writing poems at Charterhouse School where he was educated. He continued to write verse after 1914 when he saw active service with the Royal Welch Fusiliers but he did not write satisfying poems until he was middle-aged. Almost a third of the many poems Graves wrote could be classified as 'love poems'. In 1963 he confessed, 'My theme was always the practical impossibility, transcended only by miracle, of absolute love continuing between man and woman.' Apart from poetry he wrote many novels ('To make money,' he said) and an outstanding autobiography, **Goodbye to all that**.

WITH HER LIPS ONLY

This honest wife, challenged at dusk
At the garden gate, under a moon perhaps,
In scent of honeysuckle, dared to deny
Love to an urgent lover: with her lips only,
Not with her heart. It was no assignation;
Taken aback, what could she say else?
For the children's sake, the lie was venial;
'For the children's sake,' she argued with her conscience.

Yet a mortal lie must follow before dawn:
Challenged as usual in her own bed,
She protests love to an urgent husband,
Not with her heart but with her lips only;
'For the children's sake,' she argues with her conscience,
'For the children' – turning suddenly cold towards them.

Federico Garcia Lorca (1898–1936) Of all 20th-century Spanish writers Lorca is the most celebrated internationally. His plays and poems are known and revered. He was born in a village near Granada, the son of a wealthy farmer and a culturally sensitive mother who much influenced her son. At one time Lorca dreamed of being a painter and at art school he became a close friend of Salvador Dali. He was also a gifted musician. But his reputation, of course, is essentially that of a poet and dramatist – one who felt deep sympathy for the oppressed, not least the gipsy people who had settled in the caves of Sacro Monte on the outskirts of Granada. Still in his prime, Lorca, alas, was killed by Franco's fascists soon after the outbreak of the Civil War in 1936.

THE
FAITHLESS WIFE

So I took her to the river
believing she was a maiden,
but she already had a husband.

It was on Saint James's night
and almost as if I was obliged to.
The lanterns went out
and the crickets lighted up.
In the farthest street corners
I touched her sleeping breasts,
and they opened to me suddenly
like spikes of hyacinth.
The starch of her petticoat
sounded in my ears
like a piece of silk
rent by ten knives.
Without silver light on their foliage
the trees had grown larger

and a horizon of dogs
barked very far from the river.

Past the blackberries,
the reeds and the hawthorn,
underneath her cluster of hair
I made a hollow in the earth.
I took off my tie.
She took off her dress.
I my belt with the revolver.
She her four bodices.
Nor nard nor mother-o'-pearl
have skin so fine,
nor did crystals lit by moon
shine with such brilliance.

Her thighs slipped away from me
like startled fish,
half full of fire,
half full of cold.
That night I ran
on the best of roads
mounted on a nacre mare
without bridle or stirrups.
As a man, I won't repeat
the things she said to me.
The light of understanding
has made me most discreet.
Smeared with sand and kisses
I took her away from the river.
The swords of the lilies
battled with the air.

I behaved just like myself.
Like a proper gipsy.
I gave her a large sewing basket,
of straw-coloured satin,
and I did not fall in love

for although she had a husband
she told me she was a maiden
when I took her to the river.

Translated by J L Gili and Stephen Spender

Jacques Prévert (1900–77) is one of the most widely read poets in France. His book of poems, **Paroles** (1946) from which 'Breakfast' is taken, achieved phenomenal popularity. He was also a notable screen-writer, associated with such films as **Les Enfants du Paradis**. 'Breakfast' is but one of his poems where his filmic gift is evident. He has been described as the most poetical of screen-writers and the most unliterary of poets.

BREAKFAST

He put the coffee
In his cup
He put the milk
In the cup of coffee
He put the sugar
In the cup of coffee
He stirred it
With the little spoon
He drank the coffee
And he put the cup down
Without speaking to me
He lit
A cigarette
He blew rings
With the smoke
He put the ash
In the ash-tray
Without speaking to me
Without looking at me
He got up
He put
His hat on
He put his raincoat on
Because it was raining
And he went out

Into the rain
Without a word
Without looking at me
And I put
My head in my hands
And I cried

Translated by Margaret Crosland

Itzik Manger (1901–69) was born in Rumania of Yiddish-speaking parents. His first book of poems was published in 1929 and he soon gained a reputation akin to that of Dylan Thomas because of his outrageous Bacchanalian behaviour. When the Quakers had helped him to flee from the Nazis and settle in London I happened to meet him. Lubricated with vodka, he promptly punched me on the jaw because I was young and wrote poetry! Having no audience in Britain his frustration was evident. He emigrated to New York where he was celebrated by those who read Yiddish poetry and who enjoyed his charming updated biblical themes and parables.

JEALOUS ADAM

A yellow canary trilled
on a tree in paradise.
Between a song and a dream
Adam opened his eyes.

A red-hot sunray darted
across the dewy grass.
And chasing it were a weasel
and a rabbit running fast.

Adam smiled contented,
as he watched his beautiful Eve,
her body as young as the day,
beneath a covering leaf.

He looked at her and thought,
enjoying the lovely sight:
daylight is good by day,
as is the dark at night.

Then Adam rose and went
into the clamour of spring,
and in his breast he felt
the beat of every wing.

But listen! Down there in the valley
a river rushed ahead –
a little river – yet Adam,
he suddenly grew sad.

For in the water he saw
another Adam one day.
What is the Water-Adam up to,
and who is he anyway?

Perhaps it's true, perhaps it's not,
but how is one to know?
Maybe it's Adam – the other one –
who's playing with Eve just now.

He must go back at once,
and back in haste he went.
But there stood Eve and held
a cuckoo in her hand.

Tell me, she asked the bird,
whether I am really fair,
whether he truly loves me,
my husband, Adam dear?

And Adam, as he heard her voice,
did not know why it was,
he felt like burying his head
and sobbing in the grass.

Translated by Jacob Sonntag

C Day Lewis (1904–72) who assumed the pseudonym of Nicholas Blake when writing popular detective novels, was born of Anglo-Irish parentage – his mother being a descendant of Oliver Goldsmith. During the 1930s, when Day Lewis was a schoolmaster, he became associated in the minds of the poetry-reading public with young left-wing poets such as W H Auden and Stephen Spender. 'Come, Live with Me', which parodies the 16th-century love lyric of Christopher Marlowe, was written during the years of mass unemployment. After the war his poems largely ceased to reflect social concerns. He was elected Professor of Poetry at Oxford in 1951 and in 1968 was appointed Poet Laureate.

COME, LIVE WITH ME

Come, live with me and be my love,
And we will all the pleasures prove
Of peace and plenty, bed and board,
That chance employment may afford.

I'll handle dainties on the docks
And thou shalt read of summer frocks:
At evening by the sour canals
We'll hope to hear some madrigals.

Care on thy maiden brow shall put
A wreath of wrinkles, and thy foot
Be shod with pain: not silken dress
But toil shall tire thy loveliness.

Hunger shall make thy modest zone
And cheat fond death of all but bone –
If these delights thy mind may move,
Then live with me and be my love.

W H Auden (1907–73), the son of a doctor and a former nurse, gained the attention of discerning critics while he was still a student at Oxford. He was a confident youth, one who believed that on reaching crossroads the traffic lights would turn green for him. Like other poets of his generation he had left-wing sympathies and felt strongly enough about the Spanish Civil War that he went to Spain. His subsequent publications alerted the reading public to a poet of remarkable versatile talent. *Another Time* (1940) confirmed his reputation as a major poet of the 20th century. In 1939 he emigrated to the USA and seven years later became an American citizen. Both poems included here are well known – 'Lay your sleeping head' has been much anthologised and 'Stop all the Clocks' was featured in the popular film *Four Weddings and a Funeral*.

LAY YOUR SLEEPING HEAD

Lay your sleeping head, my love,
Human on my faithless arm;
Time and fevers burn away
Individual beauty from
Thoughtful children, and the grave
Proves the child ephemeral:
But in my arms till break of day
Let the living creature lie,
Mortal, guilty, but to me
The entirely beautiful.

Soul and body have no bounds:
To lovers as they lie upon
Her tolerant enchanted slope
In their ordinary swoon,
Grave the vision Venus sends

Of supernatural sympathy,
Universal love and hope;
While an abstract insight wakes
Among the glaciers and the rocks
The hermit's sensual ecstasy.

Certainty, fidelity
On the stroke of midnight pass
Like vibrations of a bell
And fashionable madmen raise
Their pedantic boring cry:
Every farthing of the cost,
All the dreaded cards foretell,
Shall be paid, but from this night
Not a whisper, not a thought,
Not a kiss nor look be lost.

Beauty, midnight, vision dies:
Let the winds of dawn that blow
Softly round your dreaming head
Such a day of sweetness show
Eye and knocking heart may bless,
Find the mortal world enough;
Noons of dryness see you fed
By the involuntary powers,
Nights of insult let you pass
Watched by every human love.

STOP ALL THE CLOCKS

Stop all the clocks, cut off the telephone,
Prevent the dog from barking with a juicy bone,
Silence the pianos and with muffled drum
Bring out the coffin, let the mourners come.

Let aeroplane circle moaning overhead
Scribbling on the sky the message He is Dead
Put crepe bows round the white necks of the public doves
Let the traffic policemen wear black cotton gloves.

He was my North, my South, my East and West,
My working week and my Sunday rest,
My noon, my midnight, my talk, my song;
I thought that love would last forever: I was wrong.

The stars are not wanted now; put out every one:
Pack up the moon and dismantle the sun;
Pour away the ocean and sweep up the woods:
For nothing now can ever come to any good.

Louis MacNeice (1907–63) The Belfast-born classical scholar and son of a Church of Ireland clergyman worked most of his adult life for BBC Radio, writing and producing acclaimed radio features. He used to be described as a dandy, but when I met him in the 1950s his appearance was akin to one of those down-at-heel ex-public schoolboys who appear in some Graham Greene novels! His poetry, however, was always elegant, charming and enjoyable, as can readily be seen in his **Collected Poems** which appeared three years after his untimely death.

MEETING POINT

Time was away and somewhere else,
There were two glasses and two chairs
And two people with one pulse
(Somebody stopped the moving stairs):
Time was away and somewhere else.

And they were neither up nor down,
The stream's music did not stop
Flowing through heather, limpid brown,
Although they sat in a coffee shop
And they were neither up nor down.

The bell was silent in the air
Holding its inverted poise –
Between the clang and clang a flower,
A brazen calyx of no noise:
The bell was silent in the air.

The camels crossed the miles of sand
That stretched around the cups and plates;
The desert was their own, they planned
To portion out the stars and dates:
The camels crossed the miles of sand.

Time was away and somewhere else.
The waiter did not come, the clock
Forgot them and the radio waltz
Came out like water from a rock:
Time was away and somewhere else.

Her fingers flicked away the ash
That bloomed again in tropic trees:
Not caring if the markets crash
When they had forests such as these,
Her fingers flicked away the ash.

God or whatever means the Good
Be praised that time can stop like this,
That what the heart has understood
Can verify in the body's peace
God or whatever means the Good.

Time was away and she was here
And life no longer what it was,
The bell was silent in the air
And all the room a glow because
Time was away and she was here.

Bernard Spencer (1909–63) A small news item appeared in the newspapers of 13 September 1963 announcing the death of Bernard Spencer at the age of 53: 'He was believed to have fallen from a train when he opened a door by mistake' the Reuters' item continued. Few reading their papers that day had ever heard of Spencer. And that, lamentably, is still the case despite the publication of his **Collected Poems** in 1981. Spencer, born in Madras, was the son of a judge. While working for the British Council in Egypt he shared a flat with his friends Lawrence Durrell and Keith Douglas, both of whom recognised that Spencer's poems could hit the bull's-eye, dead centre.

PART OF PLENTY

When she carries food to the table and stoops down
– Doing this out of love – and lays soup with its good
Tickling smell, or fry winking from the fire
And I look up, perhaps from a book I am reading
Or other work: there is an importance of beauty
Which can't be accounted for by there and then,
And attacks me, but not separately from the welcome
Of the food, or the grace of her arms.

When she puts a sheaf of tulips in a jug
And pours in water and presses to one side
The upright stems and leaves that you hear creak,
Or loosens them, or holds them up to show me,
So that I see the tangle of their necks and cups
With the curls of her hair, and the body they are held
Against, and the stalk of the small waist rising
And flowering in the shape of breasts;

Whether in the bringing of the flowers or the food
    She offers plenty, and is part of plenty,
And whether I see her stooping, or leaning with the flowers,
What she does is ages old, and she is not simply,
No, but lovely in that way.

Jean Earle (1909–2002) It is never too late to write significant poetry, as Jean Earle proved. She was 71 when her first book was published and 90 when her last one appeared. Adam Thorpe in the **Observer** remarked that her poems are 'leavened with a dry wit and her age makes her poems both imperative and moving'. Jean Earle was born in Bristol and lived most of her life in Wales. 'The May Tree' is taken from **The Sun in the West**, which was published in 1995.

THE MAY TREE

Now they are old, on dull mornings –
Nothing to get up for –
Wrinkles hardly show
Behind drawn curtains.
Under the side lamp
White hair sheens gold.

After early tea, while they keep warm
Under the duvet,
Something comes over them and they make love,
Much as when young . . .
Easing each other, without care
What 'anyone' might think
If 'anyone' knew. Why not?

Eyes without glasses see the world
Not as it is but as it was.
They find redundant, soft
Still-wild places. Their old age
Is bold as brass.

She recovers first; as women do.
He naps on.

Like a knock at the door
Comes a may tree she has
Sometimes remembered. How it went mad
With scent and snow, spending itself
On to the earth; yet there was more and more
Celebration, long after time to stop.

Next year it died.

She looks at this; and stamps on the connection,
Manfully; as women do.

Michael Burn (1912–) retired to North Wales following a distinguished career in the army and in journalism. A winner of the Keats Poetry Prize, he is a novelist and dramatist in addition to publishing four volumes of poetry. He has recently published his autobiography, **Turn Towards the Sun**. As can be seen from the following poem, he is not averse to mocking his neighbours affectionately and comically.

WELSH LOVE LETTER

Were all the peaks of Gwynedd
In one huge mountain piled,
Cnicht on Moelwyn,
Moel-y-gest, Moel Hebog,
And Eryri on top,
And all between us,
I'd climb them climb them
All!
To reach you.
O, how I love you!

Were all the streams of Gwynedd
In one great river joined,
Dwyfor, Dwyryd,
Glaslyn, Ogwen,
And Mawddach in flood,
And all between us,
I'd swim them swim them
All!
To reach you.
O, how I love you!

Were all the forts of Gwynedd
In one great fortress linked,
Caer and castle,

Criccieth, Harlech,
Conwy, Caernarfon,
And all in flames,
I'd jump them jump them
All!
To reach you.
O, how I love you!

See you Saturday,
If it's not raining.

John Frederick Nims (1913–99), born of a Catholic family in Michigan, was a much respected American poet, translator and editor. His versions of poems by St John of the Cross are much admired as is his own work. He was for some years editor of the famous magazine *Poetry* (Chicago). The love poem included here was the dedicatory poem to his wife, Bonnie, when his volume, *Selected Poems*, was published in 1982.

LOVE POEM

My clumsiest dear, whose hands shipwreck vases,
At whose quick touch all glasses chip and ring,
Whose palms are bulls in china, burrs in linen,
And have no cunning with any soft thing

Except all ill-at-ease fidgeting people:
The refugee uncertain at the door
You make at home; deftly you steady
The drunk clambering on his undulant floor.

Unpredictable dear, the taxi drivers' terror,
Shrinking from far headlights pale as a dime
Yet leaping before red apoplectic streetcars –
Misfit in any space. And never on time.

A wrench in clocks and the solar system. Only
with words and people and love you move at ease;
In traffic of wit expertly manoeuvre
And keep us, all devotion, at your knees,

Forgetting your coffee spreading on our flannel,
your lipstick grinning on our coat,
So gaily in love's unbreakable heaven
Our souls on glory of spilt bourbon float.

Be with me, darling, early and late. Smash glasses –
I will study wry music for your sake.
For should your hands drop white and empty
All the toys of the world would break.

R S Thomas (1913–2000) Welsh poet and priest, was born in Cardiff of a father who served in the merchant navy. His poetry became first admired during the 1950s when fashionable literary criticism welcomed clarity of theme and plainness of diction after the riotous and richer language of such poets as Dylan Thomas and George Barker. He received the Queen's Gold Medal for poetry as early as 1964. I once shared a platform with R S Thomas when he, as a Welsh Nationalist, indicated that he felt he was betraying Wales by writing in English. 'In writing a poem,' Thomas once declared, 'one is like a fisherman playing a fish, getting the sense of it.' Over the years his was an abundant and nutritious catch.

A MARRIAGE

We met
   under a shower
of bird-notes.
   Fifty years passed,
love's moment
   in a world in
servitude to time.
   She was young;
I kissed with my eyes
   closed and opened
them on her wrinkles.
   'Come,' said death,
choosing her as his
   partner for
the last dance. And she,
   who in life
had done everything
   with a bird's grace,
opened her bill now
   for the shedding
of one sigh no
   heavier than a feather.

John Cornford (1915–36) There are some poets whose names survive because of one single poem however many others they may have written. Cornford – who, aged 21, volunteered to fight for the International Brigade in Spain against Franco and was killed at the battle of Huesca – was one such. The poem is all the more poignant for being the last one he wrote.

POEM

Heart of this heartless world,
Dear heart, the thought of you
Is the pain at my side,
The shadow that chills my view.

The wind rises in the evening,
Reminds that autumn is near.
I am afraid to lose you,
I am afraid of my fear.

On the last mile to Huesca,
The last fence for our pride,
Think so kindly, dear, that I
Sense you at my side.

And if bad luck should lay my strength
Into the shallow grave,
Remember all the good you can;
Don't forget my love.

John Manifold (1915–85) was born in Melbourne, the eldest son of a wealthy Australian father who disinherited him. In 1934, at Cambridge, like his contemporaries, Burgess, Maclean, Philby and Blunt, he joined the Communist Party. During the Second World War he worked for British Intelligence! He married the singer Katharine Hopwood and had two children. His *Selected Verse* was published in London in 1948. He declared that his poetry is about women, horses, soldiers, revolutionists, landscapes, myths and history. During his lifetime he became an expert on Australian ballads and folk music and received a pension from the Soviet government.

SONG

My dark-headed Katchen, my spit-kitten darling,
You stick in my mind like an arrow of barley;
You stick in my mind like a burr on a bear,
And you drive me distracted by not being here.

I think of you singing when dullards are talking;
I think of you fighting when fools are provoking;
To think of you now makes me faint on my feet,
And you tear me to pieces by being so sweet.

The heart in my chest like a colt in a noose
Goes plunging and straining, but it's no bloody use;
It's no bloody use, but you stick in my mind,
And you tear me to pieces by being so kind.

Alun Lewis (1915–44) poet and short story writer, was born at Aberdare in South Wales where many a youngster was destined to become a coal miner. Lewis, however, won a scholarship to Cowbridge Grammar School and continued his education at Aberystwyth University where he studied medieval history. In 1941 he was called up for war-service and in that same year married Gweno Ellis. Soon after he was posted to India. He never came back. Like the First World War poet Edward Thomas, whom he so admired, Lewis suffered from black moods. It seems likely that Alun Lewis, lonely and dejected, shot himself – that it was not an accident as officially recorded. His two books of poems, **Raiders Dawn** and **Ha! Ha! Among the Trumpets**, give witness to an important talent prematurely lost.

GOODBYE

So we must say Goodbye, my darling,
And go, as lovers go, for ever;
Tonight remains, to pack and fix on labels
And make an end of lying down together.

I put a final shilling in the gas,
And watch you slip your dress below your knees
And lie so still I hear your rustling comb
Modulate the autumn in the trees.

And all the countless things I shall remember
Lay mummy-cloths of silence round my head;
I fill the carafe with a drink of water;
You say, 'We paid a guinea for this bed,'

And then, 'We'll leave some gas, a little warmth
For the next resident, and these dry flowers,'
And turn your face away, afraid to speak
The big word, that Eternity is ours.

Your kisses close my eyes and yet you stare
As though God struck a child with nameless fears;
Perhaps the water glitters and discloses
Time's chalice and its limpid useless tears.

Everything we renounce except our selves;
Selfishness is the last of all to go;
Our sighs are exhalations of the earth,
Our footprints leave a track across the snow.

We made the universe to be our home,
Our nostrils took the wind to be our breath,
Our hearts are massive towers of delight,
We stride across the seven seas of death.

Yet when all's done you'll keep the emerald
I placed upon your finger in the street;
And I will keep the patches that you sewed
On my old battledress, my sweet.

IN HOSPITAL: POONA (1)

Last night I did not fight for sleep
But lay awake from midnight while the world
Turned its slow features to the moving deep
Of darkness, till I knew that you were furled,

Beloved, in the same dark watch as I,
And sixty degrees of longitude beside
Vanished as though a swan in ecstasy
Had spanned the distance from your sleeping side.

And like to swan or moon the whole of Wales
Glided within the parish of my care:
I saw the green tide leap on Cardigan,

Your red yacht riding like a legend there,
And the great mountains, Dafydd and Llewelyn,
Plynlimmon, Cader Idris and Eryri
Threshing the darkness back from head and fin,
And also the small nameless mining valley

Whose slopes are scratched with streets and sprawling graves
Dark in the lap of firwoods and great boulders
Where you lay waiting, listening to the waves –
My hot hands touched your white despondent shoulders

– And then ten thousand miles of daylight grew
Between us, and I heard the wild daws crake
In India's starving throat; whereat I knew
That Time upon the heart can break
But love survives the venom of the snake.

Gavin Ewart (1916–95), born in London and Cambridge-educated, had his first book published when he was 22 years old. The second appeared when he was 50. After 1966, especially following the end of his employment in an advertising agency, his fecundity was such that a reviewer remarked that it seemed Ewart wrote two or three poems a week. 'Much more than that,' Ewart replied. In his latter years he became a star of the poetry-reading circuit: his witty, often sexually explicit, verse provoked laughter and applause. Outwardly Gavin Ewart seemed very respectable and gentlemanly. So it was always a surprise to hear him read aloud his raunchy verse. But he wrote more serious poems too, without losing his witty lightness of touch.

LOVE SONG

As you get old you begin to wonder –
what was all that lightning and thunder
actually about?
It was more than holding hands,
it had a lot to do with glands –
but now you're far out,

floating calmly in a lonely seascape;
passionate rose-garden, stormed treescape
very long ago
left behind – what they call Youth
seems now ridiculous, uncouth
(if you want to know).

As you settle into peace, or dourness,
that bitter-sweet, that sweet-and-sourness
is a vanished taste;
yet those who never clasped and kissed
don't know exactly what they missed
or what exactly went to waste.

Robert Lowell (1917–77) was born into an old aristocratic Boston family – the Lowells, it was said, talked only to the Cabots and the Cabots talked only to God! Robert Lowell was educated initially at Harvard and then at Kenyon College, Ohio, where he was influenced and helped by the poet and critic John Crowe Ransome. During the Second World War he was jailed as a conscientious objector and his pacifism later led him to protest about the war in Vietnam. Lowell's early poetry was formal and costive but with *Life Studies* (1959) he broke free from traditional restraints and soon earned the reputation of being the greatest American poet of his time.

THE OLD FLAME

My old flame, my wife!
Remember our lists of birds?
One morning last summer, I drove
by our house in Maine. It was still
on top of its hill –
Now a red ear of Indian maize
was splashed on the door.
Old Glory with thirteen stripes
hung on a pole. The clapboard
was old-red schoolhouse red.

Inside, a new landlord,
a new wife, a new broom!
Atlantic seaboard antique shop
pewter and plunder
shone in each room.

A new frontier!
No running next door
now to phone the sheriff
for his taxi to Bath
and the State Liquor Store!

No one saw your ghostly
imaginary lover
stare through the window,
and tighten
the scarf at his throat.

Health to the new people,
health to their flag, to their old
restored house on the hill!
Everything had been swept bare,
furnished, garnished and aired.

Everything's changed for the best –
how quivering and fierce we were,
there snowbound together,
simmering like wasps
in our tent of books!

Poor ghost, old love, speak
with your old voice
of flaming insight
that kept us awake all night.
In one bed and apart,

we heard the plow
groaning up hill –
a red light, then a blue,
as it tossed off the snow
to the side of the road.

John Heath-Stubbs (1918–) In one of Heath-Stubbs's poems he
states, 'Blind as a bat I've been for 30 years or more.' Maybe so but
this gifted poet sees more and is more knowledgeable than many of
his colleagues. Indeed, recondite facts often find their way into his
poems. When I was a presenter of *Poetry Please* for Radio 4 and a
poem chosen for the programme contained an arcane reference that
puzzled me, I would telephone John Heath-Stubbs and call on his
encyclopaedic knowledge. As a student at Oxford his poetry was
rather fancifully high-flown but in later years it became more
conversationally pitched, and rooted in the real world.

ADDRESS NOT KNOWN

So you are gone, and are proved bad change, as we had
    always known,
And I am left lonely in London the metropolitan city,
Perhaps to twist this incident into a durable poem –
The lesson of those who give their love to phenomenal
    beauty.

I am coming to think now that all I have loved were shadows
Strayed up from a dead world, through a gap in a raped tomb,
Or where the narcissus battens in mythological meadows:
Your face was painted upon the coffin-lid from Fayoum.

Is this my pain that is speaking? The pain was not long
    protracted:
I make a statement, forgive the betrayal, the meanness, the
    theft.
Human, I cannot suppose you had planned all that was
    enacted:
Fortitude must be procured to encounter the hollowness left.

The sun will not haver in its course for the lack of you,
Nor the flowers fail in colour, nor the bird stint in its song.
Only the heart that wanted somehow to have opened up
Finds the frost in the day's air, and the nights which appear
    too long.

William Meredith (1919–), American poet, served as a naval pilot during the Second World War. It was during that period he began writing seriously. He confessed, 'I found myself relying on my writing to make sense of an experience and a world for which nothing in a protected and rather unobservant childhood had prepared me.' After the war he studied and taught at Princeton and from 1955 at Connecticut College, New London. Over the years he has received a number of grants and fellowships in recognition of his contribution to American literature and is a Pulitzer Prize winner.

POEM

The swans on the river, a great
flotilla in the afternoon sun
in October again.

In a fantasy, Yeats saw himself appear
to Maud Gonne as a swan,
his plumage fanning his desire.

One October at Coole Park
he counted fifty-nine wild swans.
He flushed them into a legend.

Lover by lover is how he said they flew,
but one of them must have been without a mate.
Why did he not observe that?

We talk about Zeus and Leda and Yeats
as if they were real people, we identify constellations
as if they were drawn there on the night.

Cygnus and Castor & Pollox
are only ways of looking at
scatterings of starry matter,

a god putting on swan-flesh
to enter a mortal girl
is only a way of looking at love-trouble.

The violence and calm of these big fowl!
When I am not with you
I am always the fifty-ninth.

Vernon Scannell (1922–) In his autobiographical writings Vernon Scannell tells of his experiences as a wartime soldier and a professional boxer. Most of his working life, though, he has been a freelance broadcaster and writer whose poetry shows continual dexterity and inventiveness. He has taken the advice of Thomas Hardy who wrote, 'The ultimate aim of the poet should be to touch our hearts by showing his own.' He has won a number of literary awards and was granted a Civil List pension for services to literature in 1980.

NO SENSE OF DIRECTION

I have always admired
Those who are sure
Which turning to take,
Who need no guide
Even in war
When thunders shake
The torn terrain,
When battalions of shrill
Stars all desert
And the derelict moon
Goes over the hill:
Eyes chained by the night
They find their way back
As if it were daylight.
Then, on peaceful walks
Over strange wooded ground,
They will find the right track,
Know which of the forks
Will lead to the inn
I would never have found;
For I lack their gift,
Possess almost no

Sense of direction.
And yet I owe
 A debt to this lack,
 A debt so vast
 No reparation
 Can ever be made,
 For it led me away
 From the road I sought
 Which would carry me to –
 I mistakenly thought –
 My true destination:
 It made me stray
 To this lucky path
 That ran like a fuse
 And brought me to you
 And love's bright, soundless
 Detonation.

A LOVE SONG

I've always been in love with you I swear
'Impossible,' they say, yet it is true:
I speak with certainty, for I was there.

When I reeled groggy as the punchbowl air
Was spiced with melody I longed for you;
I've always been in love with you I swear.

My infant whispers to the beat-up bear
Were meant for you, the tears and kisses too;
I speak with certainty, for I was there.

Let experts, calendars and maps declare
I'm nuts or have at least one wobbly screw;
I've always been in love with you I swear.

New kinds of beauty and the wish to share
These riches were rehearsals, as I knew;
I speak with certainty, for I was there.

These shadow-loves were work-outs to prepare
For this, the main event, that they led to;
I've always been in love with you I swear;
I speak with certainty, for I was there.

Daniel Hoffman (1923–) was born in New York and attended Columbia University. After serving in the US Air Force during the war, he taught at Columbia, then at Swarthmore College before becoming Poet-in-residence at the University of Pennsylvania. In 1973–4 he was appointed Consultant in Poetry at the Library of Congress in Washington. Hoffman, who is also a formidable critic, has suggested that poetry defies desolation in that, if it is successful, it will give delight. His poems, formal or free, on occasions blossom with refreshments like the springtime magnolia trees of Swarthmore where, with his wife Elizabeth, he now lives.

A MARRIAGE

'Remember that farmer down in Maine
Who said to us, 'I've been
An abandoned island
Since she's gone'?

– That's the hurt of proud flesh
We've known,
The heart's self-borne contagion
When you or I have parted us

With those rending, furious
irretrievable accusations.
Each gulp of air keeps the wound fresh.
Left to the individual freedom

Of broken ends
We can't make meet, I roar
Off, a space-bound satellite
With no earth to encircle, adrift

In that unfinished void
Where nothing numbs the red scar
  Of a burnt-out asteroid.
  And yet I turn, seeking some tremor

  Of your light,
  Your heat,
  Wherever in that emptiness
  You are.'

John Ormond (1923–90) was born in a village near Swansea. As a young poet his work was too influenced by the poetry of his older neighbours, Dylan Thomas and Vernon Watkins. After a long silence he reinvented himself, even using a different surname. By then (1964) his poetry voice had become singularly his own. A verbally fastidious poet – he was also a gifted BBC Wales film-maker – he revised his eloquent poetry obsessively, saying, 'You cannot play a tune on a slack string.' A plaque outside the house where he lived in Cardiff signifies how highly he is regarded in his native country.

IN SEPTEMBER

Again the golden month, still
Favourite, is renewed;
Once more I'd wind it in a ring
About your finger, pledge myself
Again, my love, my shelter,
My good roof over me,
My strong wall against winter.

Be bread upon my table still
And red wine in my glass; be fire
Upon my hearth. Continue,
My true storm door, continue
To be sweet lock to my key;
Be wife to me, remain
The soft silk on my bed.

Be morning to my pillow,
Multiply my joy. Be my rare coin
For counting, my luck, my
Granary, my promising fair
Sky, my star, the meaning
Of my journey. Be, this year too,
My twelve months long desire.

DESIGN FOR A QUILT

First let there be a tree, roots taking ground
In bleached and soft blue fabric.
Into the well-aired sky, branches extend
Only to bend away from the turned-back
Edge of linen where day's horizons end;

Branches symmetrical, not over-flaunting
Their leaves (let ordinary swansdown
Be their lining), which in the summertime
Will lie quietly upon her, the girl
This quilt's for, this object of designing;

But such too, when deep frosts veneer
Or winds prise at the slates above her,
Or snows lie in the yard in a black sulk,
That the embroidered cover, couched
And applied with pennants of green silk,

Will still be warm enough that should she stir
To draw a further foliage about her
The encouraged shoots will quicken
And, at her breathing, midnight's spring
Can know new season as they thicken.

Feather-stitch on every bough
A bird, one neat French-knot its eye,
to sing a silent night-long lullaby
And not disturb her or disbud her.
See that the entwining motives run

In and about themselves to bring
To bed the sheens and mossy lawns of Eden;
For I would have a perfect thing
To echo if not equal Paradise
As garden for her true temptation:

So that in future times, recalling
The pleasures of past falling, she'll bequeath it
To one or other of the line,
Bearing her name or mine,
With luck I'll help her make beneath it.

Yehuda Amichai (1923–2000), the distinguished Israeli poet, was born in Germany but went to Israel while still a child. During the 1939–45 war he joined the Jewish Brigade in the British Army and fought against the Germans in the Egyptian Western Desert. Though he lived chiefly in Jerusalem he made many trips to the USA and Britain where translations of his poetry have been much admired. Ted Hughes wrote, 'I, for one, return to his poetry again and again and always find myself shaken, as by something truly genuine and alive.'

QUICK AND BITTER

The end was quick and bitter.
Slow and sweet was the time between us,
slow and sweet were the nights
when my hands did not touch one another in despair
but with the love of your body
which came between them.

And when I entered into you
it seemed then that great happiness
could be measured with the precision
of sharp pain. Quick and bitter.

Slow and sweet were the nights.
Now is as bitter and grinding as sand –
'We shall be sensible' and similar curses.

And as we stray further from love
we multiply the words,
words and sentences long and orderly.
Had we remained together
we could have become a silence.

Translated by Assia Gutmann

Dannie Abse (1923–) 'Epithalamion' is an early poem that I wrote while I was still a medical student. It pleases me that it is used from time to time at secular weddings. 'Epithalamion' is reprinted here at the request of the publisher.

EPITHALAMION

Singing, today I married my white girl
beautiful in a barley field.
Green on thy finger a grass blade curled,
so with this ring I thee wed, I thee wed,
and send our love to the loveless world
of all the living and all the dead.

Now, no more than vulnerable human,
we, more than one, less than two,
are nearly ourselves in a barley field –
and only love is the rent that's due
though the bailiffs of time return anew
to all the living but not the dead.

Shipwrecked, the sun sinks down harbours
of a sky, unloads its liquid cargoes
of marigolds, and I and my white girl
lie still in the barley – who else wishes
to speak, what more can be said
by all the living against all the dead?

Come then all you wedding guests:
green ghost of trees, gold of barley,
you blackbird priests in the field,
you wind that shakes the pansy head
fluttering on a stalk like a butterfly;
come the living and come the dead.

Listen flowers, birds, winds, worlds,
tell all today that I married
more than a white girl in the barley –
for today I took to my human bed
flower and bird and wind and world,
and all the living and all the dead.

John Smith (1924–) was born in High Wycombe, Bucks, and educated at St James's School, Gerrards Cross. For many years he was managing director of a literary agency. As a poet he has generally eschewed Ezra Pound's cry of 'Make it new!' But his somewhat old-fashioned, technically skilful verse has been appreciated by, among others, Philip Larkin who, as a co-judge, awarded John Smith's *Excursus in Autumn* a Poetry Book Society Choice. Fine examples of his poetry can be read in Jeremy Robson's *Poems from Poetry and Jazz in Concert*.

THE BIRTH OF VENUS

Somewhat incredible seems the fable
   Of this great lady of the sea;
Could one so flushed with love be able
   To store such rich propensity
     In that damp element, cold and dead;
     Could love arise from the grey sea-bed,
   Or rank weed nourish such potency?

Yet from that foam she, singing, sprang,
   Of beauty hitherto unknown
That at her birth the sharp stars sang.
   She on a shell was shoreward blown.
     It seems the natural order then
     Fell into chaos around her, when
   The Seasons saw her there, alone.

Naked she stood and like the dawn
   We may suppose, like the sun uprisen,
Her hair more gold than the gold corn
   Still dashed with spray from her wet prison.
     Winter, summer, autumn, spring
     Combined to greet her, caroling,
   Contracted in one sweet elision!

She then, not as one might expect,
   Being spied by strangers in such wise
Seemed not one jot perturbed, perplexed,
   That she stood naked to their eyes;
     The fresh wind made her pink flesh tingle
     Where she stepped on that hallowed shingle
   And took the slow world by surprise.

The electric sun grew hot; the rocks
   Shook where her radiance struck them there,
As when the nightingale unlocks
   With wires of song the night-shut air;
     Whatever sights her gay eyes saw,
     No matter what foul shape before,
   Grew up miraculously fair.

That such remarkable beauty should
   Without premeditation flower
Cannot, perhaps, be understood:
   Suffice to say that in one hour
     The world was changed; the earth's pulse turned
     As if Olympic Gods' fire burned
   In every field and bower.

Venus, most near and dear of all
   Those Goddesses whose lives we scan,
Keep for all time our hearts in thrall
   Wherein, at your birth, Love began.
     However great or proud he be
     Without you, Goddess from the sea,
   How pitiably small is man.

Love, like your birth, is never shown
   By signs less wonderful than these.
It is your Halcyon firebird flown
    Along our veins, else stagnant seas;
      We may not understand, nor tell
      The miracle of that rich shell
That offered up Love's mysteries.

    Therefore, miraculous Venus, lie
      About us fabulous and bland,
   Keep us forever in your eye
      And make our limbs your precious strand;
       Teach us our bliss and rule us so:
       Of Heaven or Hell, we nothing know
      Save what through Love we understand.

Peter Porter (1929–), Australian poet, was born in Brisbane. In 1951 he came to London and worked in an advertising agency that, surprisingly, employed several poets including Gavin Ewart and Peter Redgrove. Later, leaving the agency, he became a freelance writer – one with an extensive knowledge of music and painting. Intelligent and generous he is a familiar figure on the London literary scene. His poetry has won many awards. His first wife died in 1974 and that deeply unhappy event led him to write a number of moving poems published in his book *The Cost of Seriousness*, from which the following poem is taken. It refers back to John Donne's friend, Bishop King, who wrote his exequy when his young wife, Anne, died in 1664.

AN EXEQUY

In wet May, in the months of change,
In a country you wouldn't visit, strange
Dreams pursue me in my sleep,
Black creatures of the upper deep –
Though you are five months dead, I see
You in guilt's iconography,
Dear Wife, lost beast, beleaguered child,
The stranded monster with the mild
Appearance, whom small waves tease,
(Andromeda upon her knees
In orthodox deliverance)
And you alone of pure substance,
The unformed form of life, the earth
Which Piero's brushes brought to birth
For all to greet as myth, a thing
Out of the box of imagining.
This introduction serves to sing
Your mortal death as Bishop King
Once hymned in tetrametric rhyme
His young wife, lost before her time;

Though he lived on for many years
His poem each day fed new tears
To that unreaching spot, her grave,
His lines a baroque architrave
The Sunday poor with bottled flowers
Would by-pass in their mourning hours,
Esteeming ragged natural life
('Most dearly loved, most gentle wife'),
Yet, looking back when at the gate
And seeing grief in formal state
Upon a sculpted angel group,
Were glad that men of god could stoop
To give the dead a public stance
And freeze them in their mortal dance.

The words and faces proper to
My misery are private – you
Would never share your heart with those
Whose only talent's to suppose,
Nor from your final childish bed
Raise a remote confessing head –
The channels of our lives are blocked
The hand is stopped upon the clock,
No one can say why hearts will break
And marriages are all opaque:
A map of loss, some posted cards,
The living house reduced to shards,
The abstract hell of memory,
The pointlessness of poetry –
These are the instances which tell
Of something which I know full well,
I owe a death to you – one day
The time will come for me to pay
When your slim shape from photographs
Stands at my door and gently asks
If I have any work to do
Or will I come to bed with you.
O scala enigmatica,

I'll climb up to that attic where
The curtain of your life was drawn
Some time between despair and dawn –
I'll never know with what halt steps
You mounted to this plain eclipse
But each stair now will station me
A black responsibility
And point me to that shut-down room,
'This be your due appointed tomb.'

I think of us in Italy:
Gin-and-chianti-fuelled, we
Move in a trance through Paradise,
Feeding at last our starving eyes,
Two people of the English blindness
Doing each masterpiece the kindness
Of discovering it – from Baldovinetti
To Venice's most obscure jetty,
A true unfortunate traveller, I
Depend upon your nurse's eye
To pick the altars where no Grinner
Puts us off our tourists' dinner
And in hotels to bandy words
With Genevan girls and talking birds,
To wear your feet out following me
To night's end and true amity,
And call my rational fear of flying
A paradigm of Holy Dying –
And, oh my love, I wish you were
Once more with me, at night somewhere
In narrow streets applauding wines,
The moon above the Apennines
As large as logic and the stars,
Most middle-aged of avatars,
As bright as when they shone for truth
Upon untried and avid youth.

The rooms and days we wandered through
Shrink in my mind to one – there you
Lie quite absorbed by peace – the calm
   Which life could not provide is balm
   In death. Unseen by me, you look
   Past bed and stairs and half-read book
   Eternally upon your home,
   The end of pain, the left alone.
   I have no friend, or intercessor,
   No psychopomp or true confessor
   But only you who know my heart
   In every cramped and devious part –
   Then take my hand and lead me out,
   The sky is overcast by doubt,
   The time has come, I listen for
   Your words of comfort at the door,
   O guide me through the shoals of fear –
   'Furchte dich nicht, ich bin bei dir.'

Elaine Feinstein (1930–), the Lancashire-born, Cambridge-educated poet and novelist, is also the translator of a number of Russian poets and biographer of Marina Tsvetaeva. Like the work of that Russian poet, Feinstein's linguistically clean-cut poetry – she tends to disallow decorative embellishments – is essentially autobiographical and may surprise readers because of its emotional frankness. I once gave a poetry reading with Elaine Feinstein at a secure long-term prison near Stratford-upon-Avon and can vouch for the spontaneous response her love poems evoked from that unlikely captive audience.

BONDS

There are owls in the garden and a dog barking.
After so many fevers and such loss,
I am holding you in my arms tonight, as if
your whole story were happening at once:
the eager child in lonely evacuation
walking into intelligence and then
manhood when we were first *copains*,
setting up tent in a rainy Cornish field, or
hitchhiking down to Marseilles together.

You were braver than I was and so
at your side I was never afraid, looking for
Dom 99 in the snows of suburban Moscow,
or carrying letters through Hungarian customs,
I learnt to trust your intuitions more than my own,
because you could meet Nobel laureates,
tramps and smugglers with the same confidence,
and your hunches worked, those molecular puzzles,
that filled the house with clay and wire models.

In the bad times, when like poor Tom Bowling,
you felt yourself gone for ever more,
    and threw away all you deserved, you asked me
    What was it all for? And I had no answer, then
    or a long time after that madness;
    nor can I now suggest new happiness
    or hope of good fortune, other than
    staying alive. But I know that lying at your side
    I could enter the dark bed of silence like a bride.

Ruth Fainlight (1931–) was born in New York; her father was English and her mother American. She went to school in the USA and later in England, before going to art school. In 1959 she married the novelist, Alan Sillitoe, and, after some peregrine years, settled in London. Her first book of poems appeared in 1967 and other volumes have followed regularly. Her poetry has been translated into several languages and her book *Sugar-Paper Blue* was shortlisted for the Whitbread Poetry Award.

THE BETROTHAL

What is this, why do they wrestle in the grass,
Tear the clothes that separate their skins?
If she wishes to defend herself, why
Do her limbs melt, why does she strain closer?
Even the earth is more caressing than he.
Crumbling, it blots her cool from his sweat,
Its dryness soothes the chafe of their grinding.
And the rosebay-silk, whiteness unfurling
From split pods, confirms that love is precious.

And he, what is he doing? He's forgotten
Who she is. Something is pulling him down
To the earth's centre, there's an opening;
The grasses seem to be lashing his back,
Forcing him to push deeper and deeper.
Hair in his mouth and a voice distract.
The strength of this impulse to murder becomes
The fervent, whispered phrase, 'I love you'.

Somewhere else love must be real, but not here,
This is beyond them both. They search each other's
Eyes, but only find themselves, minute,
Plunging through expanded pupils to nothing.
Each iris complicated as a stellar map,

Embarked into that flecked immensity,
Empty silence echoes from the void
In answer to the question, 'Do you love me?'

The field is so deep, its soil a talc of bones,
He's far from her, out between the planets,
But his embrace makes her one with the earth.
She seeks comfort from the dead who support her.
If she could hear them talk, they might explain
What love is – or perhaps the shadow of grass
And rosebay on his back, like hieroglyphs,
Could be deciphered, if she exchange
The rest of her life as payment for the answer.

Alan Brownjohn (1931–) edited an admired small literary magazine when he was a student at Oxford and soon after he became associated with London-based poets called The Group. More than the others in that clan Brownjohn often displayed a narrative gift in his poetry, so it was no surprise when he also published novels. At one time he was a London borough councillor and a Labour parliamentary candidate. For many years he was chairman of the Poetry Society, for which he worked selflessly. At present he is a freelance writer, regularly reviewing poetry for the *Sunday Times*.

OFFICE PARTY

We were throwing out small-talk
On the smoke-weary air,
When the girl with the squeaker
Came passing each chair.

She was wearing a white dress,
Her paper-hat was a blue
Crown with a red tassel,
And to every man who

Glanced up at her, she leant over
And blew down the hole,
So the squeaker inflated
And began to unroll.

She stopped them all talking
With this trickery,
And she didn't leave out anyone
Until she came to me.

I looked up and she met me
 With a half-teasing eye
And she took a mild breath and
Went carefully by,

And with cold concentration
To the next man she went,
And squawked out the instrument
To its fullest extent.

And whether she passed me
Thinking that it would show
Too much favour to mock me
I never did know –

Or whether her withholding
Was her cruelty,
And it was that she despised me,
I couldn't quite see –

So it could have been discretion,
And it could have been disgust,
But it was quite unequivocal,
And suffer it I must:

All I know is: she passed me,
Which I did not expect
– And I'd never so craved for
Some crude disrespect.

Peter Meinke (1932–), American poet, was for many years the director of the Writing Workshop at Eckerd College in St Petersburg, Florida. With his artist wife, Jeanne Clark, he lives in a house in St Petersburg surrounded by 'the bright explosion of azaleas'. His skilful, witty poetry is too little known in Britain, though in the USA, where he contributes to the **New Yorker**, **Atlantic Monthly**, **Georgia Review** and other leading journals, it has won many prizes and awards.

HELEN

A mad sculptor in our park
has fashioned there, in writhing bronze,
the old story of Leda and the swan.
There, the trees are cool and dark
and men may sit and contemplate
the myriad forms that love can take.

And on the cement pedestal, between
the burning figures and the cool grass,
is scrawled in printing recognizably obscene,
Helen Goldberg is a good peece of ass.

Ah, Helen Goldberg, your mortal lover
has proved false, and, what is worse,
illiterate. Tell me, did he hover
swanlike above your trembling skirts
in a burst of light and shadow,
or were you surprised by a shower
of gold, shining like El Dorado
in your surrendering hour?

But probably you shifted your gum from one side
to the other while he had trouble
with his skin-tight pants (not yours)

and you hoped later he'd give you a ride
on his cycle – and anyway love's a bubble
that bursts like gum in feminine jaws.

There should be a moral here, and yet
I'd be willing to bet
there was no swan back then, either,
just a story that brown-haired Leda
made up for her mother to explain
why she was late again,
and her lovely daughter didn't hatch from an egg,
but was born in the same inelegant way
as Helen Goldberg, whose pointed breasts
and bottom-twitching walk
devastated all of 77th Street West,
Troy 23, New York.

KISSING

I remember when we used to kiss
Your eyes closed for a moment then opened as if
in wonder at the world's sweet surprises of tongues of lips

We'd sit on the edge of the forbidden bed antici-
pation bursting like cocaine *Oyesyesyes*
I *remember* when we used to kiss!

Nothing's like touch like skin on skin
and every minute the young beginning to sip
in wonder at the world's sweet surprises of tongues of lips

of taste and smell: the rollercoaster dips
of the body's bends And still through a myopic mist
I remember when we used to kiss

everywhere! lunatic lovebugs repetitive
as villanelles in your old jeep crying with bliss
and wonder at the world's sweet surprises of tongues of lips

We'd say pupils wide with excess *Do that! Do this!*
What innocence! What wickedness!
How I remember when we used to kiss
in wonder at the world's surprises: *Tongues! And lips!*

Fleur Adcock (1934–) was born in New Zealand and read classics at the Victoria University of Wellington. In 1963 she left New Zealand to settle permanently in London. For a time she worked as a librarian before becoming a freelance writer. Adcock has revealed that she began writing early, at the age of five or six. Her mature work is accessible and witty and has attracted the admiration of many discerning readers. She writes that 'The happiest state is to have just begun writing the next poem.'

PIANO CONCERTO IN E FLAT MAJOR

In her 1930s bob or even, perhaps,
if she saw something quainter as her fashion,
long thick hair in a plait, the music student
showed her composition to her tutor;
and she aroused, or this enhanced, his passion.

He quoted from it in his new concerto,
offering back to her as homage
those several bars of hers the pianist plays
in the second movement: part of what she dreamed
re-translated, marked more with his image.

But the seven steady notes of the main theme
are his alone. Did the romance go well?
Whether he married her's recorded somewhere
in books. The wistful strings, the determined
percussion, the English cadences, don't tell.

Seamus Heaney (1939–), the renowned Irish poet, is the eldest of nine children whose father was a farmer and cattle dealer. Seamus Heaney read English at Queen's University, Belfast, where he became associated with a group of poetry-writing students. Heaney tells how they used 'to talk poetry day after day with an intensity and prejudice that cannot but have left a mark on all of us'. His first book of poems, **Death of a Naturalist**, was published in 1966. It happened that I reviewed this volume and I can boast that, like others, I gave it an excellent notice! Further books of poems followed to consolidate Heaney's high reputation and this most articulate of poets was awarded the Nobel Prize for literature in 1995.

THE UNDERGROUND

There we were in the vaulted tunnel running,
You in your going away coat speeding ahead
And me, me then like a fleet god gaining
Upon you before you turned into a reed

Or some new white flower japped with crimson
As the coat flapped wild and button after button
Sprang off and fell in a trail
Between the Underground and the Albert Hall.

Honeymooning, moonlighting, late for the Proms,
Our echoes die in that corridor and now
I come as Hansel came on the moonlit stones
Retracing the path back, lifting the buttons

To end up in a draughty lamplit station
After the trains have gone, the wet track
bared and tensed as I am, all attention
For your step following and damned if I look back.

Eavan Boland (1944–) was born in Dublin, the daughter of a diplomat who became the Irish ambassador in London and later Irish representative at the United Nations. After school in London and New York, Eavan Boland attended Trinity College, Dublin. With her third book of poems, which was a Poetry Book Society choice, her high reputation as a poet extended beyond the borders of her native country. She is a member of the Irish Academy of Letters and at present teaches at Stanford University, California.

SONG

Where in blind files
Bats outsleep the frost,
Water slips through stones
Too fast, too fast
For ice, afraid he'd slip
By me I asked him first.

Round as a bracelet
Clasping the wet grass
An adder dowsed by berries
Which change blood to cess.
Dreading delay's venom
I risked the first kiss.

My skirt in my hand
Lifting the hem high
I forded the river where
Drops splashed my thigh.
Ahead of me at last
He turned at my cry:

'Look how the water comes
Boldly to my side;
See how the waves attempt

What you have never tried.'
And he late that night
Followed the leaping tide.

QUARANTINE

In the worst hour of the worst season
   of the worst year of a whole people
a man set out from the workhouse with his wife.
He was walking – they were both walking – north.

She was sick with famine fever and could not keep up.
   He lifted her and put her on his back.
He walked like that west and west and north.
Until at nightfall under freezing stars they arrived.

In the morning they were both found dead.
      Of cold. Of hunger. Of the toxins of a whole history.
But her feet were held against his breastbone.
The last heat of his flesh was his last gift to her.

Let no love poem ever come to this threshold.
   There is no place here for the inexact
praise of the easy graces and sensuality of the body.
There is only time for this merciless inventory:

Their death together in the winter of 1847.
   Also what they suffered. How they lived.
And what there is between a man and woman.
And in which darkness it can best be proved.

Tony Curtis (1946–) is one of the best poets now writing in Wales. He was born in Carmarthen and educated at University College, Swansea. His keen interest in painting and in golf is reflected in his poetry as are such themes as the consequence of war and the vagaries of family life. As well as being the author of some nine books of verse he is an energetic anthologist and a respected art critic. He is also the Professor of Poetry at the University of Glamorgan where, under his aegis, the creative writing programme has gained a fine reputation. The portrait referred to in the poem below is by the German artist, Otto Dix.

PORTRAIT OF THE PAINTER HANS THEO RICHTER AND HIS WIFE GISELA IN DRESDEN, 1933

This is the perfect moment of love –
Her arm around his neck,
Holding a rose.

Her wisps of yellow hair
The light turns gold.
Her face is the moon to his earth.

Otto's studio wall glows
With the warm wheat glow
Of the loving couple.

This is after the dark etchings,
The blown faces. This is after Bapaume –
The sickly greens, the fallen browns.

She is a tree, her neck a swan's curved to him.
His hands enclose her left hand
Like folded wings.

This before the fire-storm,
Before the black wind,
The city turned to broken teeth.

It is she who holds the rose to him,
Theo's eyes which lower in contentment
To the surgeon's smock he wears for painting.

This is the perfect moment,
The painted moment
She will not survive.

This is before the hair that flames,
The face that chars. This is before
Her long arms blacken like winter boughs.

This is the harvest of their love,
It is summer in the soul,
The moment they have made together.

From Otto's window the sounds of the day –
The baker's boy calling, a neighbour's wireless
playing marches and then a speech.

Nigel Jenkins (1949–) lives in Swansea, where he works as a freelance writer and journalist. He came to notice in 1974 when, with Tony Curtis and Duncan Bush, he shared the Welsh Arts Council first Young Poet's Prize. Apart from poetry he has written a play, **Strike a Light!**, which was staged in 1985 and a study of Welsh missionaries in India, **Gwalia in Khasia**, in 1996. Social and political themes not uncommonly find their way into his verse but I have chosen a rather delicate love poem which reminds me of the early work of the American poet, William Carlos Williams.

WILD CHERRY

Tiptoe on wall-top, head in
clouds of white blossom, I
reached for the fullest, the
flounciest sprays, I travelled
many miles to give you them.

You placed them, smiling,
in a jar on your table,
& there was beauty between us,
between us too were words,
white clouds of words . . .

One of the sprays I'd kept myself,
& I'll know on what morning
you brush up the petals, you
toss out the twigs with the ashes
& empties, yesterday's news.

Andrew Motion (1952–) It was ironic that Andrew Motion should have been chosen as Poet Laureate – that is one who is expected to produce poems on significant occasions, royal and otherwise – for he is essentially a poet most himself when focusing on personal matters, the stuff of childhood, marital life and past encounters. On the other hand, he did win the Newdigate Prize while a student at Oxford, a prize which requires a poet to have the ability to write on a given subject with true craftsmanship. He is also a commended biographer of John Keats and Philip Larkin.

ON THE TABLE

I would like to make it clear that I have bought
this tablecloth with its simple repeating pattern
of dark purple blooms not named by any botanist
because it reminds me of that printed dress you had
the summer we met – a dress you have always said
I never told you I liked. Well I did, you know. I did.
I liked it a lot, whether you were inside it or not.

How did it slip so quietly out of our life?
I hate – I really hate – to think of some other bum
swinging those heavy flower-heads left to right.
I hate even more to think of it mouldering on a tip
or torn to shreds – a piece here wiping a dipstick,
a piece there tied round a crack in a lead pipe.

It's all a long time ago now, darling, a long time,
but tonight just like our first night here I am
with my head light in my hands and my glass full,
staring at the big drowsy petals until they start to swim,
loving them but wishing to lift them aside, unbutton them,
tear them, even, if that's what it takes to get through
to the beautiful, moon-white, warm, wanting skin of you.

Carol Ann Duffy (1955–) was born in Glasgow of Irish parents and educated at Liverpool University where she studied philosophy. Recognition of her fresh and accessible poetry came early when she won awards for poets under thirty. Soon after she claimed the Dylan Thomas Award and in 1993 the Whitbread Award. Justly, she is now one of the most popular poets in Britain. In 1994 Carol Ann Duffy and I were sent on tour together by Penguin to promote our respective **Selected Poems**. After such poetry readings there were occasions when I felt myself to be merely an admiring, observing chaperone as she charmingly signed book after book!

WHO LOVES YOU

I worry about you travelling in those mystical machines.
Every day people fall from the clouds, dead.
Breathe in and out and in and out easy.
Safety, safely, safe home.

Your photograph is in the fridge, smiles when the light comes on.
All the time people are burnt in the public places.
Rest where the cool trees drop to a gentle shade.
Safety, safely, safe home.

Don't lie down on the sands where the hole in the sky is.
Too many people being gnawed to shreds.
Send me your voice however it comes across oceans.
Safety, safely, safe home.

The loveless men and homeless boys are out there and angry.
Nightly people end their lives in the shortcut.
Walk in the light, steadily hurry towards me.
Safety, safely, safe home. (Who loves you?)
Safety, safely, safe home.

VALENTINE

Not a red rose or a satin heart.

I give you an onion.
It is a moon wrapped in brown paper.
It promises light
like the careful undressing of love.

Here.
It will blind you with tears
like a lover.
It will make your reflection
a wobbling photo of grief.

I am trying to be truthful.

Not a cute card or a kissogram.

I give you an onion
Its fierce kiss will stay on your lips,
possessive and faithful
as we are,
for as long as we are.

Take it.
Its platinum loops shrink to a wedding ring,
if you like.

Lethal
Its scent will cling to your fingers,
cling to your knife.

Simon Armitage (1963–) was born in Huddersfield, West Yorkshire, and studied geography at Portsmouth Polytechnic. For a number of years he worked as a probation officer in Manchester and experiences from this period are reflected in some of his poetry. With the publication of his first book **Zoom!** (1989) he received instant and admiring attention by critics. In 1994 he became the **Sunday Times** writer of the year. Since that date books of his verse of a consistent and commendable quality have been regularly appearing.

IN OUR TENTH YEAR

This book, this page, this harebell laid to rest
between these sheets, these leaves, if pressed still bleeds
a watercolour of the way we were.

Those years: the fuss of such and such a day,
That disagreement and its final word,
your inventory of names and dates and times,
my infantries of tall, dark, handsome lies.

A decade on, now we astound ourselves;
still two, still twinned but doubled now with love
and for a single night apart, alone,
how sure we are, each of the other half.

This harebell holds its own. Let's give it now
in air, with light, the chance to fade, to fold.
Here, take it from my hand. Now, let it go.

Owen Sheers (1974–), one of the best young poets to be noticed in recent years, was born in Fiji where he spent much of his childhood before coming to Britain. He studied at Oxford before attending the Creative Writing Programme at the University of East Anglia. His first book of poems was warmly and widely reviewed and won the Vogue Talent Contest for Young Writers as well as a Gregory Award. At present he works for BBC Wales and his second book is awaited with much curiosity.

ANTONIA'S STORY

She told me how she fell to sleep with the sound of his fists
    on the door.
Dull thuds that echoed on the stairs,
that became the beat of her heart on the sheet,
the rustle of blood in her ear on the pillow, then sleep.

Of how she slept a dark sleep with only one dream,
of an apple ripening, then falling a fall.
Its loud thud echoing on in the night
in the beat of her heart on the sheet.

And how she woke to the sound of fists on the door
and how she was surprised by the persistence of love.

She told me how she answered the door, and how she
saw him over the policeman's shoulder, lying on the lawn,
and how she thought why is he lying on the lawn, so pale
    and quiet?
Why is he lying asleep and covered in dew?

And then how she saw the broken drainpipe he had tried
    to climb,
and how she knew he had fallen, ripe in the night,
from the broken drainpipe, which still swung wild,
a madman's finger preaching in the wind.

And then she told me how now each night she unlocks
    the door,
which sometimes gets blown, wild in the wind.
How her feet echo, dull on the stairs, as she climbs to bed
where she falls to sleep, the rustle of blood in her ear.

And how each night she sleeps a dark sleep with only
    one dream,
of an apple which falls, ripe in the night.
And of how she wakes with the beat of her heart on the sheet,
surprised by the persistence of love.

ACKNOWLEDGEMENTS

For permission to reprint poems in this anthology acknowledgement is made to the following:

To Mrs Hana Amichai for the poem 'Quick and Bitter' by Yehuda Amichai; To William Meredith and North Western University Press for 'Poem' from **Effort at Speech**. To Faber and Faber for 'Lay your sleeping head' and 'Twelve Songs IX' by W H Auden from **Collected Poems**; 'In Our Tenth Year' by Simon Armitage from **Kid**; 'The Old Flame' by Robert Lowell from **Selected Poems**; 'The Underground' by Seamus Heaney from **Station Island**; 'A River Merchant's Wife' by Ezra Pound from **Selected Poems**; 'On the Table' by Andrew Motion from **Salt Water**. To Seren Books for 'The May Tree' by Jean Earle from **The Sun in the West**; 'Goodbye' and 'In Hospital Poona' by Alun Lewis from **Collected Poems**; 'Antonia's Story' by Owen Sheers from **The Blue Book**. To Mrs Glenys Ormond for 'In September' and 'Design for a Quilt' by John Ormond from **Selected Poems** (Seren). To the author for 'The Portrait of Hans Theo Richter and his wife Gisela' by Tony Curtis from **War Voices** (Seren). To Elaine Feinstein for Marina Tsvetaeva's 'An Attempt at Jealousy' from **Selected Poems** (Hutchinson) and her own poem 'Bonds' from **Daylight** (Carcanet). To Ruth Sonntag for Itzik Manger's 'Jealous Adam' from **Modern European Verse** (Vista Books). To Peter Meinke for his poems 'Helen' and 'Kissing'. To Fleur Adcock for her poem 'Piano Concerto in E Flat Major' from **Selected Poems** (Oxford University Press). To Mrs Margot Ewart for 'Love Song' by Gavin Ewart from **The Ewart Quarto** (Hutchinson). To the author for 'Epithalamion' by Dannie Abse from **New and Collected Poems**

(Hutchinson). To John Heath-Stubbs for his poem 'Address Unknown' from *A Charm Against the Toothache* (Methuen). To Robson Books for 'The Birth of Venus' by John Smith from *A Landscape of My Own*. To the author for 'An Exequy' by Peter Porter from *Collected Poems* (Oxford University Press). To Carol Ann Duffy and The Anvil Press for her poems 'Who Loves You' and 'Valentine'. To Michael Burn for 'Welsh Love Letter' from *Open Day and Night*. To Nigel Jenkins for 'Wild Cherry'. To Bloodaxe Books for 'A Marriage' from *Mass for Hard Times* by R S Thomas. To Carcanet for 'Song' and 'Quarantine' from *Selected Poems* and *Code* by Eavan Boland and for 'With Her Lips Only' by Robert Graves from *Collected Poems*. To David Higham Associates for 'Meeting Point' by Louis MacNeice from *Collected Poems*. To Ruth Fainlight for 'The Betrothal' from *Selected Poems* (Sinclair-Stevenson). To Alan Brownjohn for 'Office Party' from *Collected Poems* (Hutchinson). To Vernon Scannell and Robson Books for 'No Sense of Direction' from *Collected Poems* and 'A Love Song' from *The Black and White Days*. To Daniel Hoffman for 'A Marriage' from *Hang-Gliding from Helicon* (Louisiana State University Press). To the Estate of C Day Lewis for 'Come Live with me and be my Love' from *The Complete Poems* (Sinclair-Stevenson).

Every effort has been made to obtain permission from copyright holders of poems included in this anthology. Sometimes this has not proved possible. We therefore wish to thank not only the above but also those copyright holders of poems which are included without acknowledgement.